W9-CDE-465

TOWN&COUNTRY

THE QUEEN

TOWN&COUNTRY

THE QUEEN

A LIFE IN PICTURES

VICTORIA MURPHY

INTRODUCTION BY STELLENE VOLANDES

HEARST
HOME

CONTENTS

INTRODUCTION BY STELLENE VOLANDES 6

CHAPTER ONE
A LIFE OF DUTY 8

CHAPTER TWO
HER "STRENGTH AND STAY" 30

CHAPTER THREE
FAMILY LIFE 48

CHAPTER FOUR
WOMAN OF THE WORLD 74

CHAPTER FIVE
A STAR AMONG STARS 94

CHAPTER SIX
SOVEREIGN OF STYLE 118

CHAPTER SEVEN

ALL THAT GLITTERS 142

CHAPTER EIGHT

A QUEEN'S BEST FRIENDS 168

CHAPTER NINE

A PALACE TO CALL HOME 188

CHAPTER TEN

COMMEMORATION AND CELEBRATION 214

INDEX 234

PHOTOGRAPHY CREDITS 238

MAY 6, 1935

FIRST PAGE Nine-year-old Princess Elizabeth and four-year-old Princess Margaret wave from the Buckingham Palace balcony alongside their grandparents King George V and Queen Mary. The royal family was appearing on the balcony during celebrations for the King's Silver Jubilee, marking his 25 years on the throne.

JUNE 2, 1953

TITLE PAGE The Queen in a coronation portrait taken by Cecil Beaton. She is wearing her coronation robes and the Imperial State Crown. She is holding the Sovereign's Sceptre with Cross in her right hand and the Sovereign's Orb in her left hand.

I t's no easy job being the queen of the United Kingdom of Great Britain and Northern Ireland, but somehow, Queen Elizabeth II has been doing it for nearly 70 years. Since taking the throne in 1952 after the death of her father, King George VI, Elizabeth has become the longest-reigning monarch not only in British history but also in the world today.

Her reign hasn't always been easy. As the queen, she's dealt with matters of state—as well as a personal life lived under a microscope—for seven decades, leading the United Kingdom through political and financial turmoil as well as unpleasant tabloid scandals. A series of unfortunate events in 1992, including a fire at Windsor Castle, led her to dub the year her "annus horribilis."

While others might have buckled under the stress, the Queen has endured. Despite her challenges, Elizabeth has demonstrated what's become a trademark fortitude and the quintessential British stiff upper lip—rarely offering clues to her private thoughts or acting out of character. In spite, or perhaps because, of her mystique, Elizabeth has come to occupy a singular place on the world stage: She personifies pomp and pageantry without ever being unrelatable. She is rarely out of touch with the feelings of her subjects and has demonstrated, in acts from her work as a mechanic during World War II to her heartfelt 2020 speech declaring that "we will meet again," that she shares as her own the concerns and obstacles of her people.

The reign of Elizabeth II is an incredible one to behold. From her earliest days as a monarch to the most recent, she's been a model of endurance, character, and style—indeed, one we've covered extensively in the pages of *Town & Country*—and we're thrilled to share with you this celebration of her reign in all its majesty.

Stellene Volandes
Editor in Chief, *Town & Country*

JUNE 2, 1953

Wearing the Imperial State Crown, the Queen leaves Westminster Abbey following her coronation.

A Life of Duty

"I DECLARE BEFORE YOU ALL THAT MY WHOLE LIFE, WHETHER IT BE LONG OR SHORT, SHALL BE DEVOTED TO YOUR SERVICE AND THE SERVICE OF OUR GREAT IMPERIAL FAMILY, TO WHICH WE ALL BELONG."

— Princess Elizabeth, speaking from Cape Town, South Africa, on her 21st birthday, April 21, 1947

APRIL 1945

Princess Elizabeth demonstrates her role in the Auxiliary Territorial Service during World War II. When she was 18 years old, Elizabeth trained as a driver and mechanic with the ATS, making her the first female royal to become a full-time member of the British Armed Forces. By the end of the war, she had reached the rank of junior commander.

Throughout her seven decades as monarch of the United Kingdom, Queen Elizabeth II has become celebrated around the world for her devotion to duty. The sudden death of her father on February 6, 1952, saw her become queen at the tender age of 25. Yet it was some time before that, on her 21st birthday, when she made perhaps her most notable speech, committing her "whole life" to service. This is the enduring philosophy the Queen upholds even today. Despite being well into her 90s and having had to adjust her timetable to accommodate her advancing age, she still carries out close to 300 engagements each year.

The Queen is head of state in the United Kingdom plus 15 other Commonwealth realms and head of the British Armed Forces. She also holds the titles Defender of the Faith and Supreme Governor of the Church of England. Her responsibilities put her at the heart of British national life. She receives red boxes of government papers daily, with the only exceptions being Christmas Day and Easter Sunday. She opens Parliament annually; carries out audiences, official visits, and investitures; and delivers many speeches. All told, she is patron or president of more than 600 organizations. While she now rarely makes overseas visits, she continues to travel the length and breadth of the United Kingdom. One of her most quoted remarks is, "I have to be seen to be believed."

Throughout her life, Elizabeth has understood the importance of being able to relate to her people by sharing their experiences, eagerly donning overalls to serve in the Auxiliary Territorial Service during World War II. Decades later in 2019, while honoring veterans on the 75th anniversary of the D-Day landings, the Queen proudly described how "the wartime generation—my generation—is resilient."

During the global coronavirus pandemic that took hold in 2020, she delivered a historic address to the nation and Commonwealth. Offering reassurance that better times lie ahead, the Queen evoked the wartime spirit by referencing Dame Vera Lynn's anthem "We'll Meet Again."

The once sprawling British Empire has disappeared, with nations formerly under British rule having claimed their independence. As they did so, the Commonwealth of Nations was formed, which today is a voluntary association of 54 independent countries with the Queen as its head. The Queen's recognition that monarchy must remain relevant to each generation has secured her position in the hearts of people young and old. While upholding many traditions, she has also been a force of modernization for the monarchy, presiding over the creation of the royal family's official websites and social media accounts and encouraging her children and grandchildren to forge their own paths. She has thoughtfully and diligently married the traditional and the modern to truly become a queen for all ages.

Five-week-old Princess
Elizabeth sleeps in her
mother's arms following her
christening in the private
chapel at Buckingham Palace.
She was born on April 21,
1926, at 17 Bruton Street in
London's Mayfair, the home
of her maternal grandparents.
She was christened Elizabeth
Alexandra Mary. At the time of
her birth, her parents held the
titles Duke and Duchess of York
and her grandfather was King
George V. Although she was
third in line to the throne after
her uncle and her father, it was
not anticipated that Elizabeth
would become queen. The line
of succession was expected to
remain with her uncle's side of
the family. On the death of King
George V, her uncle ascended
the throne in January 1936
and became King Edward VIII.

King George VI is joined by his family on his coronation day. Life changed dramatically for Princess Elizabeth when her uncle abdicated on December 11, 1936, a mere 11 months after he had become king, in order to marry American divorcée Wallis Simpson. Her father was crowned in his place and took the name King George VI, with her mother becoming Queen Elizabeth. The family moved into Buckingham Palace and, at the age of 10, Elizabeth became heir to the throne. She took on the role of heir presumptive rather than heir apparent, as at the time, the order of succession favored males. If her parents were to have had a son, he would have overtaken her position in line to the throne.

OCTOBER 13, 1940

Princess Elizabeth, with her sister, Princess Margaret, by her
side, gives her first official radio broadcast during World War II.
Elizabeth was 14 when she addressed the nation's evacuated
children on BBC's *Children's Hour*. "And when peace comes,
remember it will be for us, the children of today, to make the
world of tomorrow a better and happier place," the Princess said.
Elizabeth and Margaret spent most of the war years at Windsor
Castle, just over 20 miles from London, while their parents stayed
at Buckingham Palace in London. Buckingham Palace was bombed
in 1940 while their parents were in residence, and their mother,
Queen Elizabeth, said, "It makes me feel I can look the East End in
the face." With its concentration of docklands, London's East End
had suffered heavy bombings, and Queen Elizabeth boosted morale
with the many visits she made there.

APRIL 21, 1942

The royal family stands at attention on Princess Elizabeth's 16th birthday as she carries out her first official public engagement. Elizabeth was appointed colonel of the Grenadier Guards and inspected the regiment in Windsor. The moment marks her introduction to a lifetime of formal public appearances. It also highlights the significant relationship between the royals and the military. The sovereign is head of the British Armed Forces, and many members of the royal family have served in the military and hold honorary military appointments.

APRIL 21, 1947

Princess Elizabeth prepares to make what has become perhaps her most iconic speech. Elizabeth was on an official tour with her parents and sister in Cape Town, South Africa, when she turned 21. On that occasion, she delivered a radio broadcast dedicating her life to service. The speech, in which she said she would devote her "whole life" to "your service," is cited today to support the view that she will never abdicate.

1951

En route to Victoria, British Columbia, Princess Elizabeth and
Prince Philip look out from on board a Royal Navy ship. The
couple made their first official visit to Canada in 1951 on a trip that
began on October 8 and lasted just over a month. Canada remains
one of 15 countries outside the United Kingdom that are known as
Commonwealth realms, where the Queen is head of state. The other
14 are Antigua and Barbuda, Australia, The Bahamas, Barbados,
Belize, Grenada, Jamaica, New Zealand, Papua New Guinea,
St. Kitts and Nevis, St. Lucia, St. Vincent and the Grenadines,
Solomon Islands, and Tuvalu. The Queen has visited these
countries often throughout her reign, and her family members
continue to visit regularly on her behalf.

FEBRUARY 5, 1952

Princess Elizabeth views the scenery at Treetops Hotel in Kenya the day before her father died and she became queen. King George VI passed away in his sleep in the early hours of February 6, 1952; he had served as monarch for 15 years. Elizabeth spent the night that he died at the Treetops Hotel. She did not hear of her father's death until the afternoon of February 6, by which time she had relocated to nearby Sagana Lodge. It was Prince Philip who delivered the news to his wife after being informed by an aide. At 25 years old, Elizabeth was now queen. Her private secretary asked what name she wanted to take as sovereign. Some previous royals, including her father, had not used their given first names, but Elizabeth replied, "My own, of course." She cut her trip short to return home immediately.

FEBRUARY 7, 1952

Elizabeth left the United Kingdom as a princess and returns as its monarch. On February 8, she was formally proclaimed Queen Elizabeth II at St. James's Palace. She said, "My heart is too full for me to say more to you today than I shall always work, as my father did throughout his reign, to advance the happiness and prosperity of my peoples, spread as they are all the world over."

FEBRUARY 15, 1952

The new Queen Elizabeth II with her grandmother Queen Mary and her mother, now called the Queen Mother, as they mourn their father, son, and husband, respectively, at the funeral of King George VI. His coffin lay in state in Westminster Hall, in London, where more than 300,000 people came to pay their respects. The funeral service was held at St. George's Chapel, in Windsor, where the king's body was laid to rest.

JUNE 2, 1953

Soldiers march down the Mall, in London, for the Queen's coronation parade. There were 16 months between Elizabeth's accession and coronation. She was crowned before 8,251 guests at Westminster Abbey, where coronations have been held for 900 years. Hers was the first to be televised and was watched by more than 20 million people. Many people watched television for the first time in their lives that day. Almost 30,000 people took part in the Queen's procession through London, including members of the British Army, the Royal Navy, and the Royal Air Force. Cheering crowds lined the streets.

The Queen appears on the balcony of Buckingham Palace following her coronation ceremony. The Archbishop of Canterbury conducted the three-hour service, which was composed of six parts: the recognition, the oath, the anointing, the investiture (which includes the crowning), the enthronement, and the homage. The Archbishop asked the Queen whether she was willing to take the coronation oath, to which she replied, "I am willing." The Archbishop then asked three more questions about upholding her new position and the Queen assented to each one. She then laid her right hand on the Bible and said, "The things which I have here before promised, I will perform and keep. So help me God."

APRIL 1954

The Queen knights Air Marshal Claude Pelly in a public investiture ceremony held during a visit to Aden, Yemen. There are approximately 25 investiture ceremonies every year in the United Kingdom as well as occasional ceremonies overseas. The Queen's role in administering them is an important duty. A government committee decides who receives the honors for exceptional achievement or service in their fields of endeavor. Other members of her family also carry out investitures.

The Queen sits down to work with one of the red dispatch boxes containing government documents she receives daily. The boxes, which are made by the British leather goods company Barrow Hepburn & Gale, contain documents about government business, some of which require the Queen's signature as a matter of formality. These boxes are an iconic part of her role, and so she chose to be photographed with one to mark becoming the longest-reigning British monarch, in September 2015.

SEPTEMBER 20, 1967

The majestic cruise liner *Queen Elizabeth 2* towers above the crowds. Approximately 30,000 people lined the streets of Clydebank, Scotland, to see the Queen launch the ship. Designed for the transatlantic service from Southampton, England, to New York, the *QE2* set sail for her maiden voyage two years later, on May 2, 1969.

JUNE 20, 1958

Dressed in a protective suit and hard hat, the Queen prepares to go down a mine at Rothes Colliery in Fife, Scotland. Although her position often calls for tiaras and ball gowns, Elizabeth also makes hundreds of visits each year to meet ordinary working people in their homes and communities. Here, she officially declared the coal mine open.

1977

Huge crowds gather to meet the Queen as she conducts a walkabout in London for her Silver Jubilee, the 25th anniversary of her reign. The walkabout is often one of the most popular parts of royal visits, allowing the royals to personally greet as many members of the public as possible when touring a city or country. King George VI and his wife, Queen Elizabeth, conducted the first known walkabout during a visit to Canada in 1939 when they entered the crowd to greet assembled veterans. However, it wasn't until 1970 when the Queen and Prince Philip greeted well-wishers during an official tour of Australia and New Zealand that the walkabout started to become a regular feature of royal visits.

JUNE 16, 1980

The Queen holds on to her hat during a windy day at the Order of the Garter service in Windsor. The annual service honors the Knights of the Garter, members of the United Kingdom's oldest and most senior order of chivalry, founded by Edward III in 1348. Dressed in their distinctive plumed hats and velvet robes, the knights gather each year at St. George's Chapel, in Windsor, for a procession. Historically, members belonged to the aristocracy, but now, they are chosen in recognition of their public service. Today, the order includes the Queen, who is Sovereign of the Order of the Garter, several members of the royal family, selected foreign monarchs, and 24 knights.

The Queen receives a posy from a small child during a visit to Welshpool, Wales. Traveling the length and breadth of the United Kingdom to greet people forms the backbone of her public duties. Young children often present her with flowers, which she usually passes to a lady-in-waiting.

SEPTEMBER 5, 1997

The Queen and Prince Philip view the floral tributes left by members of the public after Princess Diana died. Diana's sudden death rocked the United Kingdom and the world, sparking an outpouring of grief. At the time of the Princess's death, the Queen was at Balmoral Castle in Scotland with Princes William and Harry, where she remained for several days. However, it soon became clear that many members of the public believed she should return to London and be more visible at this time of national mourning. There was also controversy that no flag was being flown at half-mast over the palace to honor Diana. The flagpole was empty, as tradition dictated that the Royal Standard be flown only when the monarch is in residence. This is virtually the only moment during the Queen's reign when her actions were out of step with the sentiment of her people. In the end, Elizabeth bent to their will, came back to London, and addressed the nation. The Queen also agreed that the Union Jack would be flown at half-mast over the palace on the day of the Princess's funeral. Since then, the Union Jack is flown from the palace when the Queen is away and has been flown at half-mast on occasions of mourning, such as royal deaths and terror attacks. The Royal Standard is never flown at half-mast because when a king or queen dies, they are immediately succeeded by an heir and there is always a sovereign.

OCTOBER 14, 2002

The Queen plants an oak tree at Rideau Hall, in Ottawa, Ontario, Canada. Tree planting is an integral part of royal work and often marks the occasion of a royal visit with a permanent memento. While there is no official tally, the Queen has likely planted thousands of trees throughout her reign. In 2019, at age 93, she was offered the opportunity to allow someone else to do the honors at an event. She responded, "No, no, I can still plant a tree."

MAY 2011

The Queen hosts United States President Barack Obama during
a state visit. An important part of the Queen's role as head of state
involves hosting overseas dignitaries. A formal ceremonial military
welcome is traditionally followed by a lavish state banquet that
evening in the Buckingham Palace ballroom. The Queen approves
and personally inspects every element of the banquet, from the
menus to the seating plan.

The Queen proceeds through the splendid Royal Gallery at the state opening of Parliament. One of the monarch's most important ceremonial functions is to formally open Parliament, which involves her traveling to the Palace of Westminster by coach and processing through the Royal Gallery to the House of Lords. The Queen sits on the throne in the House of Lords chamber and reads a speech prepared by the government outlining plans for the next session of Parliament. In the United Kingdom's constitutional monarchy, the Queen has no political power, but according to parliamentary guidelines, she can "advise, encourage, and warn ministers in private." She holds weekly meetings with the prime minister for most of the year. Once both houses of Parliament have passed a bill, it is given royal assent by the Queen to become law. This matter is considered a formality.

Proving she truly is a queen for the modern era, the Queen sends her first tweet. During her engagement at the Science Museum in London, the Queen posted this online message, which read, "It is a pleasure to open the *Information Age* exhibition today." The tweet was signed "Elizabeth R." The *R* stands for *Regina*, which means "Queen" in Latin. The Queen's presence online reflects the fact that she has presided over the royal family's embrace of the internet. All members of her family use social media to promote their work, and they now employ staff to manage and provide content for their online platforms.

SEPTEMBER 9, 2015

Peering out the window of a steam train, the Queen views the crowds on the historic day she became the longest-reigning British monarch, surpassing her great-great-grandmother, Queen Victoria, who reigned for 63 years, seven months, and two days. It may have been a milestone moment for the Queen and country, but it was also a working day for her, like any other: The Queen opened the new Borders Railway, in Scotland. Elizabeth said in a speech that she had "never aspired" to the record.

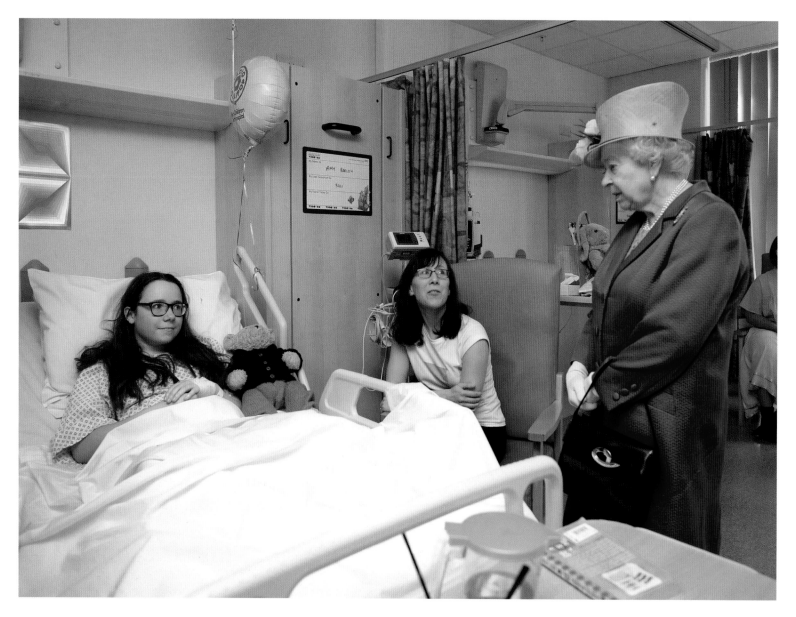

MAY 25, 2017

The Queen stands at the bedside of 12-year-old Amy Barlow, who was injured during a terror attack in the city of Manchester. It is important to Elizabeth to show solidarity and empathy with her people during times of distress. As well as issuing messages of condolences, she has often met directly with the victims of tragic events to express her sorrow personally. She also referred to this terror attack in her Christmas broadcast that year, saying, "The patients I met were an example to us all, showing extraordinary bravery and resilience."

2017

Perched at a desk in the 1844 Room at Buckingham Palace, the Queen delivers her annual Christmas broadcast. Originally recorded for radio, the broadcasts have been televised since 1957. They are taped in advance and aired in the United Kingdom at 3 p.m. on Christmas Day annually. The only exception was in 1969, when the royals took part in a fly-on-the-wall television documentary. The Queen is thought to have believed that the royal family had been seen on-screen enough that year, so she instead wrote a Christmas message. The Queen uses the Christmas Day broadcast to sum up themes of the year, and she always finishes by wishing the nation a happy Christmas.

APRIL 5, 2020

The Queen gives a televised address to the nation and Commonwealth during the coronavirus pandemic. Offering reassurance and hope, the monarch said, "We will succeed—and that success will belong to every one of us. We should take comfort that while we may have more still to endure, better days will return: We will be with our friends again; we will be with our families again; we will meet again." She also thanked all frontline workers battling the virus. Outside of her annual Christmas broadcast, the four-minute message was only the fifth time in her reign that the Queen addressed her people in a televised broadcast. The other four were during the Gulf War, in 1991; after Princess Diana's death, in 1997; on the death of the Queen Mother, in 2002; and during her Diamond Jubilee, the celebrations for the 60th anniversary of her reign, in 2012. The coronavirus message, described as "deeply personal" by palace aides, was the first time the Queen had given such an address during a global crisis.

Her "Strength and Stay"

"I THINK THE MAIN LESSON THAT WE HAVE LEARNT IS THAT TOLERANCE IS THE ONE ESSENTIAL INGREDIENT OF ANY HAPPY MARRIAGE.... YOU CAN TAKE IT FROM ME THAT THE QUEEN HAS THE QUALITY OF TOLERANCE IN ABUNDANCE."

— Prince Philip, at a celebratory golden wedding anniversary lunch, November 19, 1997

NOVEMBER 2007

The Queen and Prince Philip pose for a photograph at Broadlands, a country estate in Hampshire, England, where they spent part of their honeymoon in 1947. The palace released the image to commemorate their diamond (60th) wedding anniversary.

One person has been a constant presence by the Queen's side. Just as Queen Elizabeth II is the longest-reigning British monarch, Prince Philip holds the record as the longest-serving consort. The couple has been married for more than 70 years, and theirs was a love match right from the start. "She never looked at anyone else," the Queen's cousin Margaret Rhodes wrote in her memoir, *The Final Curtsey*.

Their first proper encounter was in 1939, when the young naval cadet Prince Philip of Greece and Denmark was asked to entertain 13-year-old Princess Elizabeth and her sister, Princess Margaret, while their parents toured Britannia Royal Naval College, in Dartmouth, southwestern England. During World War II, Elizabeth and Philip began regular correspondence, and a romance blossomed. However, it wasn't until after Elizabeth turned 21 that Buckingham Palace announced their engagement, in July 1947. They were married a few months later, in November, and Philip was given the title Duke of Edinburgh.

Philip gave up his promising military career to support his wife, and he told the BBC many years later that "nobody had much idea" of what his work should be. "There was no precedent. If I asked somebody, 'What do you expect me to do?' they all looked blank. They had no idea," he told the broadcaster in an interview to mark his 90th birthday, in 2011.

Nevertheless, he threw himself into his role, eventually becoming patron or president of more than 780 organizations. Once describing himself as "the world's most experienced plaque-unveiler," Prince Philip carried out 22,191 engagements and gave 5,493 speeches before his retirement, in August 2017. He became concerned about the environment long before those views were fashionable, and he also showed a keen interest in sports and industry. Perhaps his most notable endeavor is his eponymous initiative, The Duke of Edinburgh's Award, founded in 1956, which has engaged millions of young people around the world in 144 nations. Participants compete for bronze, silver, and gold awards by completing various challenges in volunteering, skills, physical recreation, and expedition.

Philip is known for having a no-nonsense attitude, both in public and behind closed doors. During official visits over the years, he has made many blunt, sometimes witty, and occasionally offensive remarks that are famously referred to as his gaffes. Following his retirement, he is rarely seen in public. However, he remains the Queen's steadfast companion behind the scenes. Their relationship was perhaps best summed up by Lord Charteris, the Queen's former private secretary, who told author Gyles Brandreth, "Prince Philip is the only man in the world who treats the Queen simply as another human being. He's the only man who can. Strange as it may seem, I believe she values that."

JULY 1922

Prince Philip at age one. He was born Prince Philip of Greece and Denmark on June 10, 1921, on the Greek island of Corfu. He is the only son of Prince Andrew of Greece and Denmark and Princess Alice of Battenberg and had four older sisters. In September 1922, as defeat loomed in the Greco-Turkish War, a military revolt forced Philip's uncle King Constantine I of Greece to abdicate his throne. Philip's family fled to France, with baby Philip transported in a wooden fruit box. They settled in Paris. Philip was initially educated at The Elms, an American school. In 1928, he was sent to live in England with his maternal relatives, the Mountbattens, and attend Cheam School in Cheam, Surrey.

JULY 1935

Prince Philip, at age 14, dresses for Gordonstoun School's production of *Macbeth*. In 1933, he briefly attended Schule Schloss Salem boarding school in south Germany before transferring to Gordonstoun School in Scotland. German educator Kurt Hahn established both schools, and his teachings had a big influence on Philip. Philip's mother was diagnosed with schizophrenia in 1930 and placed in a sanatorium, and it is understood that he had little contact with her for much of his childhood. When asked by the BBC in an interview for his 90th birthday whether his childhood was unsettling, Philip bluntly replied, "Well, I just lived my life—I haven't been trying to psychoanalyze myself all the time."

A 13-year-old Princess Elizabeth (seated, third from left) focuses her attention ahead, while 18-year-old naval cadet Prince Philip (standing, far right) converses behind her at the Britannia Royal Naval College, in Dartmouth. Prince Philip had been charged with entertaining the young princesses, Elizabeth and Margaret. This was Philip and Elizabeth's first substantive encounter, although they are third cousins through their mutual ancestry to Queen Victoria and both attended the same wedding in 1934. Elizabeth's governess Marion Crawford wrote about their time together in Dartmouth in her book, *The Little Princesses*: "At the tennis courts, I thought he showed off a good deal, but the little girls were much impressed. Lilibet said, 'How good he is, Crawfie. How high he can jump.' She never took her eyes off him the whole time." The following day, Philip joined the royal family for lunch, and Crawford recalled how Elizabeth "sat, pink-faced, enjoying it all very much."

OCTOBER 26, 1946

Princess Elizabeth walks with her family and Philip (far right) at the wedding of Lady Patricia Mountbatten to Lord Brabourne at Romsey Abbey, in Hampshire. Elizabeth and Philip had been in contact during the war years. Philip visited Windsor Castle, where the royal sisters stayed during the war, and watched them perform in a pantomime. Following the war, he began to visit Elizabeth regularly at Buckingham Palace. Governess Marion Crawford wrote about Philip, "He loved her very much. He was a forthright and completely natural young man, given to say what he thought. There was nothing of the polished courtier about him." By October 1946, there was much public speculation about their relationship. Photographs of Elizabeth and Philip chatting together before Lady Mountbatten's wedding as they entered the abbey for the service fueled the gossip. Philip was seen helping Elizabeth and Margaret with their coats, which further spurred speculation about them.

JULY 10, 1947

Princess Elizabeth and Prince Philip sit for an official photograph the day after the announcement of their engagement, on July 9, 1947. It is widely believed that they secretly became engaged in 1946. However, King George VI is understood to have asked that the couple wait until after Elizabeth was 21 to formalize the engagement. During that waiting period, Philip renounced his Greek and Danish titles, became a naturalized British citizen, and took the surname of his uncle Louis, 1st Earl Mountbatten of Burma. Mountbatten was also a distant cousin to Elizabeth and was a statesman and British Royal Navy officer. The official engagement announcement from the palace said that "the King has gladly given his consent" to the union.

NOVEMBER 19, 1947

Prince Philip enjoys himself with friends at his stag party. He had two stag parties: one the night before the wedding at the Dorchester Hotel in London that the media was invited to photograph (shown here) and the other a private party on November 14 with his closest friends at the Belfry Club in London. Philip and many of his friends were members of the Thursday Club, which met weekly for lunch at a restaurant in London's Soho. His best man was the aristocrat David Mountbatten, 3rd Marquess of Milford Haven, who served in the Royal Navy. Other friends included society photographer Baron Nahum and expressionist painter Feliks Topolski.

NOVEMBER 20, 1947

Princess Elizabeth and Prince Philip pose for photographs on their wedding day. They were married at 10:30 a.m. before 2,000 guests at Westminster Abbey. The event was also broadcast by BBC radio to 200 million people around the world. Elizabeth had eight bridesmaids, including her sister, Princess Margaret. On the morning of the wedding, Philip asked his cousin Patricia Mountbatten, "Am I being very brave or very foolish?" Upon the marriage, he was given the primary title of Duke of Edinburgh along with the titles Earl of Merioneth and Baron Greenwich, of Greenwich in the county of London. It was not until 10 years later, in 1957, that Philip was officially made a prince of the United Kingdom, when the Queen issued a special document, known as a letters patent, to that effect.

NOVEMBER 20, 1947

Princess Elizabeth arrives at Westminster Abbey with her father on her wedding day. They traveled in the Irish State Coach to the service, which was officiated by Geoffrey Fisher, the Archbishop of Canterbury. King George VI wrote to his daughter afterward, "When I handed your hand to the Archbishop, I felt I had lost something very precious. You were so calm and composed during the service and said your words with such conviction that I knew everything was all right." After the service, a reception was held at Buckingham Palace. The couple received more than 2,500 presents and 10,000 telegrams of congratulations. According to details released by the royal household, gifts included a bookcase from Queen Mary and a picnic case from Princess Margaret. The presents were put on display at St. James's Palace, where the public could view them.

NOVEMBER 1948

ABOVE Well-wishers outside Buckingham Palace wait for the official announcement of the birth of Prince Charles. Almost exactly a year after they married, Elizabeth and Philip welcomed their first child. Charles was born at Buckingham Palace on November 14, 1948. Like many fathers of that era, Philip was not present for the birth and is instead believed to have been playing squash with his private secretary Mike Parker. As a boy, Charles was born heir apparent. At this time, the family lived in Clarence House, in London, and would move into Buckingham Palace when Elizabeth became queen.

NOVEMBER 1947

OPPOSITE The newlyweds look at their wedding photos on their honeymoon. The couple spent their wedding night at Broadlands, in Hampshire, the home of Louis, 1st Earl Mountbatten of Burma, Philip's uncle. The rest of their honeymoon was spent at Birkhall, on the Balmoral Estate, in Scotland. In a letter to her parents while on her honeymoon, Elizabeth wrote how she and Philip "behave as though we had belonged to each other for years." He also wrote to his mother-in-law not long after they were wed, declaring, "Cherish Lilibet? I wonder if that word is enough to express what is in me."

OCTOBER 20, 1949

Prince Philip poses in his naval uniform. After attending Gordonstoun, Philip began training with the Royal Navy. He graduated from Britannia Royal Naval College and served in the British forces during World War II. Philip was mentioned in dispatches after manning searchlights during the Battle of Cape Matapan in 1941. He later wrote about the incident in the foreword of a book called *Dark Seas*, published in 2012: "I reported that I had a target in sight and was ordered to 'open shutter.'" Philip went on to describe how "hell broke loose" as the guns began firing at the cruiser, which "disappeared in an explosion and a cloud of smoke."

NOVEMBER 1949

Princess Elizabeth and Prince Philip in Malta. The couple resided on the island on and off between 1949 and 1951 when Philip was posted there with the Royal Navy. They resided in the Villa Guardamangia and attended dances with other military families. This was a rare period when Elizabeth was able to live like a normal naval wife. Philip was a first lieutenant when he was initially posted to Malta; in 1950, he was promoted to lieutenant commander and then placed in charge of HMS *Magpie*. He left active service prematurely and abruptly in July 1951 as the health of King George VI started to deteriorate rapidly. Elizabeth had already begun to take on more of her father's royal duties, most notably standing in to take the salute in Trooping the Colour, an annual event to mark the official birthday of the British sovereign, in June 1951. In September 1951, the King had an operation to remove part of his lung.

FEBRUARY 3, 1952

Princess Elizabeth and Prince Philip attend a polo match in Nyeri, Kenya, during an official visit to the country. It turned out to be just days before her father died after suffering from lung cancer. Elizabeth left for Kenya as a princess and returned to the United Kingdom as its queen. In her memoir *Daughter of Empire*, Pamela Mountbatten, Elizabeth's lady-in-waiting, recalled how it was Philip who broke the news of King George VI's death to Elizabeth, in the garden of a Kenyan lodge. She wrote how Elizabeth "remained completely calm and said simply, 'I am so sorry. This means we all have to go home.'"

JUNE 2, 1953

Prince Philip kneels before his wife at her coronation. During the ceremony, he wore a coronet and robe over his naval uniform. The service saw him pay homage to his wife and promise to be her "liege man of life and limb." As chair of the Coronation Commission, Philip was also involved in organizing the event.

DECEMBER 1953

Prince Philip walks behind his wife as they arrive in Suva, Fiji, during their six-month Commonwealth tour. Between November 1953 and May 1954, the couple traveled more than 40,000 miles by land, sea, and air touring 13 Commonwealth countries. In an era when most people did not have access to television, these personal visits were even more important to establish a bond between the royal family and the people. In public, Philip has often walked a few steps behind his wife; however, it has often been said that things were rather different in private. "Elizabeth wore the crown, but Philip wore the trousers," author Gyles Brandreth wrote in *Philip & Elizabeth: Portrait of a Marriage.*

LEFT The Queen and Prince Philip play with their children Prince Charles and Princess Anne at Balmoral Castle, in Scotland. The couple welcomed their second child, Anne, into the world on August 15, 1950. She was born third in line to the throne, but as the order of succession then favored male heirs, Anne was later overtaken in the line of succession by her younger brothers, Andrew and Edward. Philip's children did not take his surname, Mountbatten, and instead were given the surname Windsor, which King George V had adopted. However, in 1960, it was declared in the Privy Council that direct descendants without royal styles and titles would use the name Mountbatten-Windsor. This is the surname the Duke and Duchess of Sussex, Prince Harry and Meghan, gave their son, Archie, in 2019.

1955

RIGHT Prince Philip enjoys his recreational time. In his youth, Philip was a keen polo player. He took part in the sport for some 20 years before retiring in 1971, when he took up carriage riding. He championed the activity and continued to ride well into his 90s. He also enjoyed flying and gained his Royal Air Force wings in 1953, his helicopter wings in 1956, and his private pilot's license in 1959. In addition, Philip has written extensively on the environment and technology and is the author of several books. He has a strong interest in engineering and told BBC Radio 4 in 2016, "Everything not invented by God is invented by an engineer."

BELOW The Queen and Prince Philip share a moment of laughter. Their mutual sense of humor throughout the years has often been cited as one of the secrets to their successful marriage.

JUNE 25, 1960

ABOVE Prince Philip visits a school in Eastbourne where students are taking part in The Duke of Edinburgh's Award activities. Those running the organization have hailed his patronage as crucial. However, in his typical modest style, he told the BBC in 2011, "I've got no reason to be proud of it. It's satisfying that we've set up a formula that works—that's it."

OCTOBER 27, 1965

RIGHT Prince Philip stands in uniform with his uncle Louis, 1st Earl Mountbatten of Burma (left), a significant influence on his life. Philip lived with the Mountbattens for several years before his marriage to Princess Elizabeth. Mountbatten is credited with helping matchmake the relationship and was an important confidant and mentor to the young Prince Charles. In August 1979, Mountbatten and his grandson Nicholas Knatchbull, 14, were killed along with crew member Paul Maxwell, 15, when their fishing boat was blown up on the coast of Mullaghmore, County Sligo, Ireland, by the Irish Republican Army. Another passenger, the dowager Lady Brabourne, died the next day.

The Queen and Prince Philip at Windsor Castle with their four children. The Queen is often described as having had two families, as there is a 10-year gap between her second child, Princess Anne, and her third, Prince Andrew. By the time Andrew and her fourth child, Prince Edward, were born, Elizabeth was more settled in her role as sovereign, and many observers have cited how she was able to enjoy spending more time with them.

The Queen and Prince Philip share a rare public display of affection as she boards a plane from Ottawa, Ontario, for London. The couple was visiting Canada for the Proclamation of the Constitution Act.

AUGUST 22, 1972

Prince Philip barbecues as daughter Princess Anne assists during the royal family's summer holiday at Balmoral Castle, in the Scottish Highlands. Philip did not hold the traditional role of breadwinner but threw his efforts into running the family estates. In a 2008 ITV documentary, he said, "When the Queen succeeded, we sort of chatted about who would do what, I suppose. I thought that if I could relieve her of the management of the estates, it would save a lot of time." He has also been a force for the modernization of the monarchy and was the first royal to give a television interview, in 1961.

APRIL 12, 2006

Prince Philip and grandsons Prince William and Prince Harry during Harry's passing out parade following the completion of his training at the Royal Military Academy Sandhurst. Philip's grandchildren speak highly of him and have gone on to champion causes, such as the environment and sport, that Philip himself started supporting decades ago. William has described him as a legend, and Harry observed about his grandparents in a 2012 BBC documentary, "Regardless of whether my grandfather seems to be doing his own thing, sort of wandering off like a fish down the river, the fact that he's there—personally, I don't think that she could do it without him, especially when they're both at this age."

AUGUST 2, 2017

Prince Philip waves farewell to his official duties. His final engagement was on the forecourt of Buckingham Palace. He gave his last salute to the Royal Marines outside the palace at age 96, after having been their captain general for more than 64 years. When it was announced Philip would be retiring, someone said to him, "I'm sorry to hear you're standing down." Philip replied, "Well, I can't stand up much longer." Since retiring, he has been seen only occasionally in public, at events such as family weddings.

MAY 19, 2018

Prince Philip (third from left) and the Queen attend the wedding of Prince Harry to Meghan Markle. Philip's appearance was notable because just six weeks earlier, he underwent a hip replacement operation. It was one of several hospital stays for Philip throughout his 90s. In December 2011, he had a stent fitted for a blocked coronary artery. The following June, he missed part of the Queen's Diamond Jubilee celebrations after being taken to the hospital with a bladder infection. And in 2013, he underwent what the palace described as an "exploratory operation" on his abdomen. Philip was also hospitalized for four nights in December 2019 and discharged on December 24 to join his family for Christmas.

CHAPTER THREE

Family Life

"LIKE ALL THE BEST FAMILIES, WE HAVE OUR SHARE OF ECCENTRICITIES, OF IMPETUOUS AND WAYWARD YOUNGSTERS, AND OF FAMILY DISAGREEMENTS."

— The Queen, a remark reportedly made during a private conversation, 1989

MAY 1956

The Queen and Prince Philip with Prince Charles at seven years old and Princess Anne at five years old. The family enjoyed the day in Windsor Great Park, where Philip played polo.

With four children, eight grandchildren, and many great-grandchildren, as well as hundreds of other relatives, the Queen is at the heart of her large family. Many of the family traditions she observes are ones she enjoyed as a little girl with her parents, her sister, Princess Margaret, and her grandparents. These include summers spent at the family's Scottish retreat, Balmoral Castle. There, the royals enjoy active outdoor country pursuits, such as walking, horseback riding, barbecuing, country dancing, and, more controversially, grouse shooting. Despite her position, the Queen appreciates simple pleasures and has even been known to wash the dishes.

Every Christmas, the family gathers on the Sandringham Estate, in Norfolk, with events including a black-tie dinner on Christmas Eve, lunch on Christmas Day, and a shooting party on Boxing Day (December 26). Personal or humorous presents are given rather than lavish gifts, with a leopard-print bath mat and a "grow your own girlfriend" kit reportedly among the gifts exchanged. The festive season is also one of the rare moments during the year when the entire family is seen together publicly, when they make their way to church on Christmas morning.

Like all families, the royals are no strangers to disagreements and have had their fair share of ups and downs throughout the years. Unhappy marriages and affairs have played out in the glare of the spotlight, with the Queen's youngest son, Prince Edward, the only one of her four children who has not been divorced. And while the public will never truly know exactly what goes on behind closed doors, the family continues to be dogged by reports of fallouts and feuds among its members. However, the Queen remains both respected and adored by her children and grandchildren and their families.

"She always leaves a little gift or something in their room when we go and stay, and that just shows her love for her family," Kate, the Duchess of Cambridge, told a 2016 ITV documentary about the Queen's relationships with Prince George and Princess Charlotte.

Prince William showed just how much he looks up to the Queen when he said during a BBC interview ahead of her 90th birthday, "The Queen's duty and her service, her tolerance, her commitment to others—I think that's all been incredibly important to me, and it's been a real guiding example of just what a good monarch could be."

And Prince Harry told ABC News in 2012, "Behind closed doors, she's our grandmother. It's as simple as that."

1933

Princess Elizabeth plays with her doll on the grounds of the Royal Lodge, in Windsor. She enjoyed a happy childhood and was known as Lilibet to those closest to her. The Royal Lodge was the family's country retreat from 1931, and when King George VI died in 1952, the Queen Mother made it her Windsor residence until her death in 2002. It has been leased to Prince Andrew since 2003. For her sixth birthday, Elizabeth was given a miniature thatched cottage, Y Bwthyn Bach, or "The Little House," by the people of Wales. The Royal Collection Trust describes the house as being complete with electric lighting and running water as well as cutlery, utensils, and furniture. It was installed on the grounds of the Royal Lodge, where it remains today. The family's main home was a large townhouse at 145 Piccadilly in central London and was described by governess Marion Crawford as "a homelike and unpretentious household" in her book, *The Little Princesses.* Crawford wrote of taking the sisters out to explore the city, including traveling on the London Underground.

JUNE 1934

Princess Elizabeth walks with her grandparents King George V and Queen Mary. Elizabeth had an affectionate relationship with the King, whom she called Grandpa England. When Elizabeth's parents toured Australia and New Zealand in 1927, when she was a baby, she was cared for by her grandparents and her nanny Clara Knight, who was known as Allah.

Queen Elizabeth, Princess Elizabeth, and Princess Margaret enjoy the grounds of Windsor Castle. The Princesses were educated at home and learned French, history, art, and music. When it became apparent that she would one day become queen, Elizabeth received schooling in constitutional history and law. She had tutoring sessions with the vice provost of Eton and studied religion with the Archbishop of Canterbury. The palace created a Girl Guides group, which Elizabeth and Margaret joined along with their friends and the daughters of palace staff.

DECEMBER 21, 1941

Performing a pantomime at Windsor Castle, Princess Elizabeth plays Prince Charming while Princess Margaret takes on the role of Cinderella. Throughout their time at Windsor Castle during World War II, the sisters made friends with other village and evacuated children. Their former governess Marion Crawford wrote in *The Little Princesses*, "It was amusing and no doubt very instructive for the two princesses to mingle with the children there, for if among the children of court and other officials there had been a tendency to let them have an advantage, win a game, or be relieved of the more sordid tasks, there was nothing of the kind now." At Christmas, they acted in pantomimes alongside other children. Crawford, whom the royal sisters referred to as Crawfie, worked for the family for 17 years but was ostracized after her book was published in 1950.

The royal family relaxes at the Royal Lodge, in Windsor. They were a close family, with the King affectionately referring to them as "we four." Despite their busy schedules, King George VI and his wife always made sure they saw their children in the mornings and evenings. "Nothing was ever allowed to stand in the way of these family sessions," wrote Marion Crawford.

OCTOBER 21, 1950

The royal family poses for photographs after Princess Anne's christening. The photograph shows four generations of the family: Queen Mary, Queen Elizabeth, Princess Elizabeth and her husband, Prince Philip, and their children Prince Charles and Princess Anne. Charles and Anne were just three and one when their mother became queen. Almost two years later, in November 1953, the Queen and Prince Philip embarked on a six-month tour of the Commonwealth, leaving their children in the care of the Queen Mother and staff. Charles was close to his grandmother, saying on her death in 2002, "She was quite simply the most magical grandmother you could possibly have, and I was utterly devoted to her."

JUNE 13, 1951

The Queen with Princess Margaret and Group Captain Peter Townsend at Royal Ascot. Margaret fell in love with Townsend, who was an equerry to her father, King George VI, and later her sister, the Queen. He was 16 years her senior and married with two children, but he divorced his wife in 1952. He proposed to Margaret in 1953; however, at the time, the Church of England was opposed to divorce. The Queen's approval was needed for the marriage, and she asked her sister to wait for at least a year. In October 1955, Margaret announced in a statement that she would not marry Townsend, saying, "I have been aware that, subject to my renouncing my rights of succession, it might have been possible for me to contract a civil marriage. But mindful of the Church's teaching that Christian marriage is indissoluble, and conscious of my duty to the Commonwealth, I have resolved to put these considerations before any others."

1952

OPPOSITE The Queen, Prince Charles, and Princess Anne enjoy family time at Balmoral Castle, in Scotland. During their annual summer holiday in the Scottish Highlands, they have the opportunity to relax and unwind in private. The Queen takes a break from public duties during her summer in Balmoral, although she traditionally hosts prime ministers there in September.

1957

The Queen drives her children Prince Charles and Princess
Anne in Windsor. Although she is always driven to official
engagements, Elizabeth enjoys being behind the wheel when
she has the opportunity and continues to drive in her 90s.

The Queen with Prince Andrew and Prince Edward. In a 2002 BBC interview, Princess Anne hit back at critics who suggested the Queen's role implied she was a distant and uncaring mother: "We, as children, may have not been too demanding, in the sense that we understood what the limitations were in time and the responsibilities placed on her as monarch in the things she had to do and the travels she had to make. But I don't believe that any of us for a second thought she didn't care for us in exactly the same way as any other mother did. I just think it's extraordinary that anybody could construe that that might not be true."

1969

The Queen has lunch with Prince Philip, Prince Charles, and Princess Anne. The scene was filmed for the BBC documentary *Royal Family*. The program revealed the family going about their daily lives and exchanging small talk during official visits. It was hugely popular and had an estimated audience of 350 million people worldwide. Not long after, however, the film was locked away and could no longer be viewed in its entirety. Princess Anne later admitted in a 2002 BBC interview that she "never liked the idea" of the documentary.

The Queen invests Prince Charles as the Prince of Wales during a ceremony at Caernarfon Castle, in Wales. Charles was made Prince of Wales when he was nine, but he was not formally invested until he was 20. The title is given to the eldest son of kings and queens, and Charles has been the longest-serving Prince of Wales. The investiture ceremony is like a coronation, with the Prince being presented with the symbols of the position: the sword, coronet, ring, rod, and mantle. The service was televised and watched by 500 million people around the world.

Prince Edward lies on the roof of the royal family's car as the Queen, Prince Philip, and Prince Andrew stand below. The family was attending the Royal Windsor Horse Show. The Queen holds a camera to take her own pictures, something she enjoys doing in her spare time.

APRIL 1973

The Queen Mother, Princess Margaret, and the Queen attend the Badminton Horse Trials. Elizabeth remained close to her mother and sister throughout their lives. When Elizabeth became Queen in 1952, the Queen Mother and Princess Margaret moved out of Buckingham Palace and into Clarence House. In May 1960, Margaret married photographer Antony Armstrong-Jones at Westminster Abbey in the first royal wedding to be televised. They had two children together but later announced their divorce in 1978. Margaret had an infamous romance with gardener Roddy Llewellyn for close to a decade in the 1970s. For many years, the Princess led a decadent lifestyle and was a heavy drinker and smoker. She often spent time at her home on the private Caribbean island Mustique. She died on February 9, 2002, at the age of 71, after suffering from a stroke. A few weeks later, on March 30, the Queen Mother also passed away, at the age of 101, after suffering from a chest infection.

JULY 1976

Princess Anne, at the age of 25, competes as a member of the British equestrian team in the 1976 Olympic Games. The Queen opened the Games in Montreal, and the whole family came to cheer Anne on. She was the first member of the royal family to participate in the Games and rode the Queen's horse Goodwill in the equestrian three-day event. Anne passed on her love of horseback riding to her daughter, Zara, who competed in the 2012 Olympic Games in London, winning a silver medal.

JULY 29, 1981

The bridal party gathers at Buckingham Palace on Prince Charles and Lady Diana Spencer's wedding day. The wedding of the heir to the throne took place at St. Paul's Cathedral, in London, and was celebrated around the world. Billed as the "wedding of the century," crowds of around 600,000 lined the streets of London for the marriage while an estimated 750 million people worldwide watched the event on television. However, there were ominous signs about the future of the relationship early on. During their engagement interview, when asked if they were in love, Charles answered, "Whatever 'in love' means." They announced their separation in 1992—the same year a tell-all book was published detailing Princess Diana's unhappiness within the royal family. In 1995, a palace spokesman said, "The Queen wrote to both the Prince and Princess earlier this week and gave them her view, supported by the Duke of Edinburgh, that an early divorce is desirable." Charles and Diana divorced in 1996.

SEPTEMBER 17, 1982

Prince Andrew (left) returns from the Falkland Islands. The Queen welcomed her second son when he came home from serving in the Falklands war between the United Kingdom and Argentina. During the conflict, he flew a Sea King helicopter and acted as a decoy to protect warships from missile attacks. He ended his Royal Navy career in 2001, after 22 years. Andrew is often referred to as the Queen's favorite son, and she has shown her support for him throughout several controversies. In 2019, Andrew took the unprecedented move of stepping down from royal duties. It followed the fallout from his disastrous BBC Television interview in which he attempted, and failed, to explain away his controversial friendship with convicted sex offender Jeffrey Epstein.

JUNE 1987

The Queen with four-year-old Prince William and two-year-old Prince Harry in the Royal Box at Guards Polo Club in Windsor Great Park. The Queen has often been photographed relaxing with her family watching polo throughout the years.

JANUARY 3, 1988

Prince Charles, Princess Diana, the Queen, and Prince Philip watch as the royal children play on a fire engine. The Queen's grandchildren adore her and have also spoken of having a deep respect for her. Prince William told ABC News in 2012, "As I learned from growing up, you don't mess with your grandmother." In 2016, he also recounted an anecdote to Sky News about how he and cousin Peter Phillips chased Peter's sister, Zara, into a lamppost on a go-kart: "I remember my grandmother being the first person out at Balmoral running across the lawn in her kilt," he said, continuing, "[She] came charging over and gave us the most almighty bollocking, and that sort of stuck in my mind from that moment on."

AUGUST 4, 1990

Prince Edward, the Queen, Princess Diana, the Queen Mother, Prince Charles, and Princess Margaret gather outside Clarence House, in London, on the Queen Mother's 90th birthday. The event was marked officially with a pageant at Horse Guards Parade and a gala concert at the London Palladium.

SEPTEMBER 4, 1997

The Queen, Prince Philip, Prince Charles, Prince William, Prince Harry, and Peter Phillips view the floral tributes left outside Balmoral Castle, in Scotland, following Princess Diana's death on August 31, 1997. The Queen remained at Balmoral with her grandsons despite criticism that she should return to London and address the nation's mourning. In the 2017 BBC documentary *Diana, 7 Days*, which marked the 20th anniversary of the Princess's death, William said how the Queen "felt very torn between being a grandmother to William and Harry and her Queen role." He also said, "At the time, my grandmother wanted to protect her two grandsons and my father as well." The Queen returned to London and addressed the nation from Buckingham Palace on September 5, 1997, beginning, "What I say to you now, as your queen and as a grandmother, I say from my heart."

Members of the royal family convene on the steps of St. George's Chapel, in Windsor, following the wedding of Prince Edward to Sophie Rhys-Jones. Edward is the only one of the Queen's children not to get divorced. He and Sophie, who became the Earl and Countess of Wessex on their marriage, continue to carry out full-time royal duties. They have two children: Lady Louise Mountbatten-Windsor, born on November 8, 2003, and James Mountbatten-Windsor, Viscount Severn, born on December 17, 2007. In an interview with the *Sunday Times Magazine* in 2020, Sophie said about her children, "We try to bring them up with the understanding they are very likely to have to work for a living."

JUNE 14, 2003

The Queen with Prince William and Prince Harry on the balcony of Buckingham Palace following her official birthday parade, Trooping the Colour.

Prince Charles and Camilla Parker Bowles arrive for their wedding at the Windsor Guildhall. Camilla became the Duchess of Cornwall on her marriage. The couple, who were both divorced, were married in a civil service followed by a blessing at St. George's Chapel, Windsor Castle. The Queen and Prince Philip did not attend the wedding but were at the blessing. Once reviled as the "other woman" in Charles and Diana's marriage, Camilla has gradually become more accepted by the public. At the couple's wedding reception at Windsor Castle, the Queen made a touching speech, during which she said, "My son is home and dry with the woman he loves." A few months after the wedding, Prince Harry gave an interview to mark his 21st birthday and said Camilla was "not the wicked stepmother." He described her as "a wonderful woman, and she's made our father very, very happy, which is the most important thing."

APRIL 12, 2006

Prince Harry tries not to laugh as his grandmother the Queen inspects his passing out parade at the Royal Military Academy Sandhurst. The Prince enjoys a warm relationship with his grandmother, although he confessed in an interview for the 2016 BBC documentary *Elizabeth at 90: A Family Tribute,* "I always view her as my boss."

Prince William and Kate Middleton walk down the aisle of Westminster Abbey after saying their marriage vows. Once married, they became the Duke and Duchess of Cambridge. Kate's full name is Catherine and this is how the palace always refers to her. However, the public and the media generally call her Kate, which is how she first became known to the world when she became William's girlfriend. After the service, the Queen hosted a reception for 600 guests at Buckingham Palace. William told an ITV documentary in 2012 that his grandmother had offered helpful advice about the guest list: "Start from your friends, and then we'll add those we need to in due course. It's your day." The couple moved into Kensington Palace and have three children: Prince George, born on July 22, 2013; Princess Charlotte, born on May 2, 2015; and Prince Louis, born on April 23, 2018.

JUNE 13, 2012

The Queen and the Duchess of Cambridge share some levity during Elizabeth's Diamond Jubilee year visit to Nottingham. The Queen frequently undertakes official visits alongside other members of her family. They praise her devotion to duty and have often spoken of how they learn from her. "I would like to take all of her experiences, all of her knowledge and put it in a small box and to be able to constantly refer to it," William told ITV in 2012. And in a 2016 ITV documentary, Kate described the Queen's "gentle guidance."

JUNE 4, 2015

The Queen with Princess Anne (second from left) and the Countess of Wessex (far right) at an event to mark the centenary of the Women's Institute at London's Royal Albert Hall. The monarch made a speech in which she described the community organization as a constant, adding, "In 2015, it continues to demonstrate that it can make a real difference to the lives of women of all ages and cultural backgrounds, in a spirit of friendship, cooperation, and support." The Queen became a member of the Women's Institute's Sandringham branch in 1943 and continues to visit annually.

JULY 5, 2015

The Queen bends down to talk to great-grandson Prince George at Princess Charlotte's christening. In a 2016 interview for the ITV documentary *Our Queen at Ninety,* the Duchess of Cambridge said, "George is only two and a half, and he calls her Gan-Gan." Shortly before George's birth in 2013, the Queen gave royal assent to the Succession to the Crown Act, which granted males and females equal rights to the throne. Because George was a boy, the new law had no practical impact on his position. However, the change became relevant when Princess Charlotte was born in 2015, followed by Prince Louis in 2018. Under the old rules, Louis would have overtaken Charlotte to become fourth in line to the throne, but because of the new act, she has been able to hold on to her position ahead of him.

DECEMBER 25, 2017

Prince Harry, Meghan Markle, the Duke and Duchess of Cambridge, and members of the royal family walk past the crowds on the way to church on Christmas morning in Sandringham, Norfolk. This annual tradition is one of the few times the whole family gets together. In 2017, Meghan became the first royal fiancée to join the festivities, ahead of her wedding to Prince Harry the following year.

Meghan Markle, accompanied by Prince Charles, walks down the aisle of St. George's Chapel, in Windsor, to marry Prince Harry. The bride's future father-in-law stepped in to walk with her when her own father, Thomas Markle, was unable to attend the wedding. The newlyweds were given the titles Duke and Duchess of Sussex on their marriage. The couple made it clear early on that they wanted to do things their own way, opting not to appear before the world's press after their son, Archie Harrison Mountbatten-Windsor, was born on May 6, 2019. Instead, they allowed just a handful of media to be present for the first images and footage of their newborn. On January 8, 2020, they released a statement saying that they would step back as senior members of the royal family. The announcement left the rest of the royals disappointed, with the Queen issuing a rare personal statement saying, "Although we would have preferred them to remain full-time working members of the royal family, we respect and understand their wish to live a more independent life as a family while remaining a valued part of my family."

The royal family gathers on the balcony of Buckingham Palace for the Queen's official birthday parade, Trooping the Colour. This is one of the few times throughout the year that the whole family is seen together in public, and the occasion is filled with pomp and pageantry. There is much excitement when royal children make their first appearance on the palace balcony during Trooping, which is always held on a Saturday in June. There are no designated spots, but the Queen usually stands in the center. During the family appearance in 2016, she scolded Prince William to "stand up" when he knelt to talk to Prince George.

More than 1,400 soldiers, 200 horses, and 400 musicians from the Queen's personal troops, the Household Division, take part in the performance at Horse Guards Parade in Whitehall, London. Each year, a different regiment parades, or "troops," its flag, from which the ceremony derives its name. The tradition goes back to the time when flags were often paraded to help soldiers recognize their regiment's colors on the battlefield. The ceremony is believed to have started under the reign of King Charles II, in the 1600s, and has been used to mark the official birthday of the sovereign since 1748. During the parade, the Queen is greeted with a salute and carries out an inspection of the troops. The event culminates with a flyover from the Royal Air Force as the royals watch from the palace balcony.

CHAPTER FOUR

Woman of the World

"I RECALL, TOO, THE VERY MANY HAPPY VISITS TO YOUR COUNTRIES AND THE OPPORTUNITIES THEY HAVE GIVEN ME TO MARVEL AT NEW DEVELOPMENTS AS WELL AS TO DRAW INSPIRATION FROM OLD TRADITIONS."

—The Queen, on opening the Commonwealth Heads of Government Meeting in Australia, March 2, 2002

FEBRUARY 1947

Princess Elizabeth plays tag on board
HMS *Vanguard* during the royal family's
tour of South Africa.

Queen Elizabeth II is the most traveled British monarch in history, having visited 117 countries. On the eve of her 90th birthday, it was calculated that the Queen's official travels during her reign had amounted to more than one million miles—the equivalent of circumnavigating the globe 42 times. The Queen travels without a passport. The royal household's website says, "As a British passport is issued in the name of Her Majesty, it is unnecessary for the Queen to possess one." Other family members do have passports.

The Queen's ability to travel more efficiently than any king or queen before her has undoubtedly been due to the advances made in air travel throughout her reign. However, for a span of more than four decades, many of the Queen's trips were made by sea, on the *Royal Yacht Britannia*. The ship sailed more than one million nautical miles and called at more than 600 ports. The vessel served as a floating palace, which allowed Elizabeth to stop in far-flung places and play hostess wherever she went. The Queen once described *Britannia* as the "one place where I can truly relax."

Many of the Queen's trips have been to the 15 countries outside of the United Kingdom where she is head of state. In her position as head of the Commonwealth of 54 nations, she has also visited many other Commonwealth countries that have their own heads of state. Commonwealth realms Canada, Australia, and New Zealand are her most visited destinations, and she has also undertaken many trips to the Caribbean, where she remains queen of several countries.

Dispatched far and wide by the British government, the Queen holds a politically neutral position that gives her a particularly special diplomatic ability. She became the first British monarch to go to China, in 1986, an important visit following negotiations over the return of Hong Kong. In 2011, she became the first British monarch to be a guest of the Republic of Ireland since its independence. Her grandfather King George V was the last monarch to visit the country, in 1911, when it was still part of the United Kingdom.

More recently, Elizabeth's advancing years have seen her stay closer to home. Her last official overseas trip was to Malta in 2015. Members of the royal family now frequently step in to represent her at events abroad. However, her record as the most traveled British monarch is likely to endure for many decades to come.

1947

Princess Elizabeth (center) and Princess Margaret during the royal family's tour of South Africa. The Princesses traveled with their parents, King George VI and Queen Elizabeth. It was the first time a monarch took their entire immediate family on an official visit. The sisters were photographed traveling on a royal train across the country and enjoying some free time at Bonza Bay Beach, on South Africa's Eastern Cape. The trip was notable because it was where Elizabeth made her now iconic 21st birthday speech, promising to devote her "whole life" to duty.

1954

The Queen and Prince Philip arrive at Parliament House in Hobart, Tasmania, Australia, during their six-month Commonwealth tour, from November 1953 to May 1954. This was Elizabeth's first major journey as monarch, and the royal couple visited 13 countries and traveled more than 40,000 miles. Five-year-old Prince Charles and three-year-old Princess Anne remained at home in the care of the Queen Mother and staff.

APRIL 1954

The Queen and Prince Philip arrive in the Cocos (Keeling) Islands. This Indian Ocean destination was one of the final stops on their Commonwealth tour before the couple reunited with their children.

APRIL 14, 1954

Prince Charles and Princess Anne on board the *Royal Yacht Britannia* as the ship begins her maiden voyage, taking the royal children from Portsmouth to Malta and then to Tobruk, Libya, where they were reunited with the Queen and Prince Philip following their six-month Commonwealth tour. The Queen launched *Britannia* from the John Brown & Company shipyard in Clydebank, Scotland, on April 16, 1953. The ship was the last of 83 specially commissioned royal yachts, a tradition that first began in the 1660s and ended with *Britannia*'s decommissioning in 1997.

MARCH 18, 1972

The Queen relaxes on board the *Britannia*. Both the Queen and Prince Philip had a say in the design of the yacht, and the vessel was complete with state apartments, including a state dining room and a drawing room. One of the Queen's favorite spots was the more modest sun lounge, where she would take breakfast and afternoon tea. This photograph was part of a series released to commemorate Elizabeth and Philip's silver wedding anniversary.

OCTOBER 1957

The Queen shakes hands with President Dwight Eisenhower during a visit to the White House. This was Elizabeth's first official visit to the United States as monarch, and Eisenhower was the first president she met in that role. The Queen had met President Harry Truman when she was a princess visiting Washington, D.C., in 1951. She has since met every president except Lyndon Johnson.

OCTOBER 13, 1957

The Queen greets Canada's veterans at a war memorial in Ottawa, Ontario. This visit was her first to the country since becoming monarch. Canada is the country she has visited the most—a total of 22 times since becoming queen. The royal family's special relationship with Canada blossomed when King George VI and his wife, Queen Elizabeth, toured the country in 1939. It was a hugely successful visit, and Queen Elizabeth is said to have declared, "Canada made us." Following her visit in 1957, the Queen said in her Christmas broadcast, "Once again, I was overwhelmed by the loyalty and enthusiasm of my Canadian people."

JANUARY 25, 1961

RIGHT The Queen visits the Taj Mahal during her first visit to India. The British ruled what is now most of modern India, Pakistan, and Bangladesh from 1858 until independence was gained in 1947. The Queen's father, King George VI, retained the title Emperor of India until June 1948. After gaining independence from the United Kingdom, India and Pakistan joined the Commonwealth. After Bangladesh became an independent nation in 1971, it also joined the Commonwealth.

Prince Charles and Princess Diana enjoy the *Royal Yacht Britannia* at the start of their honeymoon cruise. Theirs was one of four royal honeymoons spent on the yacht. The other three were those of Princess Margaret and Antony Armstrong-Jones, Princess Anne and Captain Mark Phillips, and Prince Andrew and Sarah Ferguson. The yacht was used for official visits and was a home away from home for the royals. The Queen and Philip used to travel with their children and grandchildren on an annual yachting holiday to the islands off the west coast of Scotland. Children on board were assigned a member of the crew to entertain them, and on warm days, there was even a wading pool on the deck. Princess Anne once said, "There was so much to do; we expended so much energy that we couldn't describe our time on the yacht as a rest."

FEBRUARY 27, 1966

OPPOSITE BELOW The Queen and Prince Philip participate in a procession through the streets of Nassau, The Bahamas, during a tour of the Caribbean that was filmed for a television documentary. Elizabeth remains queen of nine Commonwealth realms in the region: Antigua and Barbuda, The Bahamas, Barbados, Belize, Grenada, Jamaica, St. Kitts and Nevis, St. Lucia, and St. Vincent and the Grenadines.

OCTOBER 20, 1973

RIGHT Large crowds gather as the Queen officially opens Australia's iconic Sydney Opera House, which was designed by architect Jørn Utzon and took 14 years to construct. Elizabeth observed, "The Sydney Opera House has captured the imagination of the world, though I understand that its construction has not been totally without problems." She added, "The human spirit must sometimes take wings or sails and create something that is not just utilitarian or commonplace."

FEBRUARY 1979

BELOW Camels pace alongside the Queen's vehicle as she is transported through the city of Al Ain in the United Arab Emirates. This was the Queen's first state visit to the UAE, where she was hosted by Sheikh Zayed bin Sultan Al Nahyan.

A crowd welcomes the Queen as she arrives in Malawi during a tour that also saw her stop in Tanzania, Botswana, and Zambia. This was the Queen's only official trip to Malawi; however, many members of her family have since visited. Prince Harry spent several weeks there in the summers of 2016 and 2017 taking part in conservation projects. African countries have played a big part in the lives of many members of the royal family. Prince William proposed to Kate Middleton in Kenya, and Prince Harry has described Botswana as his "second home." Harry also cofounded the charity Sentebale in memory of Princess Diana in the African country Lesotho to help children affected by HIV and AIDS.

OCTOBER 1986

The Queen looks closely at the Terracotta Army soldiers at the Museum of Qin Terracotta Warriors and Horses, in China's Shaanxi Province. She became the first British monarch to visit China. The trip came two years after the United Kingdom had formally committed to handing back sovereignty of Hong Kong in 1997.

FEBRUARY 1986

The Queen tours New Zealand. During this visit, protesters threw eggs at her. She was reported to have said, "I myself prefer my New Zealand eggs for breakfast." Several Commonwealth realms have questioned whether to retain the Queen as their head of state. In 1999, Australia held a referendum on whether to replace the monarch with a president. Almost 55 percent voted to keep her as their head. In 2012, Jamaica's prime minister stated her government's intent to make the country a republic, but this has yet to happen. In September 2020, Barbados announced it intends to remove the Queen as its head of state by November 2021.

OCTOBER 20, 1988

Flamenco dancers entertain guests at the Alcázar palace in Seville during the Queen and Prince Philip's state visit to Spain. This was a historic first visit to Spain by a reigning British monarch, and the couple was greeted by King Juan Carlos and Queen Sofia. In reference to the two countries' ongoing dispute over the sovereignty of Gibraltar, according to the *New York Times*, the Queen said, "We are confident that our growing mutual understanding will enable us to deal with the one remaining problem which exists between us."

MARCH 1995

The Queen with anti-apartheid heroes President Nelson Mandela (right) and Archbishop Desmond Tutu (left) during a visit to South Africa. This was the Queen's first visit to the country since 1947 and marked South Africa's rejoining the Commonwealth in 1994 after ending apartheid. South Africa had left the Commonwealth in 1961 after pressure from other member states over its apartheid policies. Following a 1960 referendum, in which only white South Africans were allowed to vote, a narrow majority of just over 52 percent chose to become a republic; the country no longer recognized the Queen as head of state. In a speech at Buckingham Palace in 2010, the Queen recalled her 1995 visit: "We could see for ourselves how much the country had changed. Just one year after the momentous elections which had brought President Mandela to power, a new atmosphere of self-confidence and positive hopes for the future was already very apparent."

DECEMBER 11, 1997

The Queen dabs her eye as she says goodbye to *Royal Yacht Britannia* during her decommissioning.
This moment is often cited as one of the few times the Queen has shed a tear in public. *Britannia* had
set sail on her farewell tour around the United Kingdom on October 20, 1997. The Queen had a last
lunch on board the vessel before the decommissioning service. In a letter for the ceremony, she wrote,
"Looking back over 44 years, we can all reflect with pride and gratitude upon this great ship which
has served the country, the Royal Navy, and my family with such distinction. *Britannia* has provided
magnificent support to us throughout this time, playing such an important role in the history of the
second half of this century." While primarily used by the royal family, *Britannia* was also employed
by politicians for trade missions and was dispatched to evacuate refugees from war-torn South Yemen
in 1986. The yacht is now moored in Edinburgh, Scotland, as a tourist attraction. All clocks on board
are set to 15:01, which is when the Queen stepped ashore for the last time.

MARCH 1, 2002

The Queen and Prince Philip watch a ceremonial fire being lit during a performance at Tjapukai Aboriginal Cultural Park. The royal couple traveled through Australia during the Queen's Golden Jubilee year, the 50th anniversary of her reign. It was on this trip that Philip asked one of the park founders, "Do you still throw spears at each other?" The infamous remark was widely viewed as a blunder; William Brim, to whom Philip was speaking, said he was not offended. The Queen's most recent visit to Australia was in 2011, when she and Philip traveled there for the Commonwealth Heads of Government Meeting in Perth.

MAY 7, 2007

The Queen and Prince Philip wave from the balcony of the White House alongside President George W. Bush and First Lady Laura Bush. This was Elizabeth's most recent trip to the United States. During the visit, she teased the president after he mistakenly announced that she had helped celebrate the United States Bicentennial in 1776 rather than 1976. In a speech, the Queen quipped, to laughter, "I wondered whether I should start this toast saying, 'When I was here in 1776,' but I don't think I will."

NOVEMBER 24, 2010

OPPOSITE The Queen observes girls reading the Koran as she visits Abu Dhabi's Sheikh Zayed Grand Mosque during an official tour of the United Arab Emirates. The British royal family regularly visits countries in the Middle East. In 2014, Prince Charles made his 10th official journey to Saudi Arabia and his fifth to Qatar. In 2019, Prince William toured Kuwait and Oman. He also became the first royal to make an official visit to Israel and the West Bank in June 2018. This was followed by a visit to the area from Prince Charles in January 2020.

MAY 20, 2011

Dressed in bright green, a deliberate choice of color to honor her hosts, the Queen walks past the Rock of Cashel, in County Tipperary, during her state visit to the Republic of Ireland. In 2011, Elizabeth became the first British monarch to visit Ireland in 100 years and the first ever since Ireland fought for and won its independence from the United Kingdom. During the four-day trip, she took part in a wreath-laying ceremony at Dublin's Garden of Remembrance to honor those who died fighting for Irish independence. She also visited Croke Park, the sports stadium near Dublin where 14 people were killed by British forces during a Gaelic football match on November 21, 1920. In a speech at a banquet at Dublin Castle, the Queen said, "With the benefit of historical hindsight, we can all see things which we would wish had been done differently or not at all."

JUNE 24, 2015

The Queen pays her respects at Berlin's Neue Wache, the Central Memorial of the Federal Republic of Germany for the Victims of War and Dictatorship. During this four-day trip to Germany, the Queen made her first visit to a World War II concentration camp. She and Prince Philip met survivors and liberators of Bergen-Belsen, where the teenage Anne Frank was among many thousands of Jewish prisoners to be murdered. The Queen said to one person, "It's difficult to imagine, isn't it?" The trip was her fifth state visit to Germany.

NOVEMBER 28, 2015

Elizabeth waves to British Royal Navy crew members during a visit to Malta for the Commonwealth Heads of Government Meeting. The Queen said in a speech during the event, "Prince Philip and I first came to live here in 1949, the same year in which the Commonwealth was founded. The 66 years since then have seen a vast expansion of human freedom: the forging of independent nations and new Commonwealth members, many millions of people sprung from the trap of poverty, and the unleashing of the talents of a global population."

APRIL 19, 2018

The Queen poses for a group photograph with Commonwealth leaders at the Commonwealth Heads of Government Meeting at Buckingham Palace. CHOGM is a biannual meeting of leaders from Commonwealth nations that member states take turns to host. The Queen has been head of the Commonwealth since coming to the throne in 1952, although the position is not a hereditary one. During CHOGM 2018, Prince Charles was approved as the Queen's designated successor as head of the Commonwealth.

CHAPTER FIVE

A Star Among Stars

"BUT LET US NOT TAKE OURSELVES TOO SERIOUSLY. NONE OF US HAS A MONOPOLY OF WISDOM, AND WE MUST ALWAYS BE READY TO LISTEN AND RESPECT OTHER POINTS OF VIEW."

— The Queen, during her Christmas broadcast, December 25, 1991

OCTOBER 1952

The Queen departs the Empire Theatre in London's Leicester Square after attending the Royal Film Performance of *Because You're Mine*.

Prince William told the BBC in a 2012 documentary that the Queen "doesn't care for celebrity." However, for many, she is the ultimate star on the global stage, even among the many world-famous people she has met.

The Queen has reigned throughout the tenure of 14 British prime ministers, from Winston Churchill to Boris Johnson, and 13 United States presidents, from Harry Truman to Donald Trump. She has hosted and greeted iconic figures including five popes, Nelson Mandela, and Mother Teresa. Over the years, she has met with the world's most eminent explorers, scientists, humanitarians, artists, and sports figures—often to honor them for their achievements.

Despite the gravity of her position, the Queen has found time to embrace the lighter side of life. She has been entertained by celebrated performers and artists worldwide, often while helping raise funds for her many charitable organizations. She is known to be fond of show tunes, and the musical *Oklahoma!* is understood to be a particular favorite. For decades, the annual Royal Variety Performance and Royal Film Performance have seen the Queen mingle with the biggest stars of stage and screen.

One of the most depicted figures worldwide, the Queen has sat for portraits by numerous artists, from Cecil Beaton to Lucian Freud, as well as been the subject of many unofficial artistic works. Her image and life story continue to inspire numerous portrayals in literature, theater, film, and television.

Prominent celebrities often seem a little nervous to meet her—and even members of her own family admit to feeling similarly. "If you suddenly bump into her in the corridor, don't panic. I know you will. We all do!" Prince Harry told a group of visitors to the palace in a 2018 ITV television series, *Queen of the World.*

Another grandchild, Princess Eugenie, summed up the Queen's effect on other people, saying in a BBC documentary to mark the Diamond Jubilee, the 60th year of Elizabeth's reign, "Whenever Granny walks into a room, everyone stands up, stops, and kind of just watches her....And I find that incredible."

Princess Elizabeth and Prince Philip pose for a photograph with their entourage, Swiss Guards, and officials of the Vatican following their audience with Pope Pius XII. This was Elizabeth's first of five visits to the Vatican. She also hosted Pope John Paul II in 1982 and Pope Benedict XVI in 2010 in the United Kingdom. The Queen holds the titles Defender of the Faith and Supreme Governor of the Church of England and, as monarch, has sworn to maintain the Church of Scotland. While Elizabeth is Anglican, she also plays an important role in celebrating religious diversity throughout the United Kingdom and the Commonwealth and has met with leaders of many different faiths.

OCTOBER 27, 1952

The Queen shakes hands with actor Charlie Chaplin at the Empire in London as she and Princess Margaret meet the stars of the film *Because You're Mine* following the annual Royal Film Performance. This was Elizabeth's first Royal Film Performance as queen; she first attended the event, which raises money for a charity that helps film industry workers in need, as a princess in 1946. Members of the royal family continue to attend the event today.

1953

The Queen chats with Prime Minister Winston Churchill, with Prince Charles and Princess Anne by her side. Churchill served as the first of her 14 prime ministers, with Boris Johnson being the most recent. As sovereign, the Queen has no political power and remains politically neutral. However, she holds weekly meetings with her prime ministers and can advise, encourage, and warn ministers on government matters. David Cameron, her 12th prime minister, said during a 2012 BBC documentary about the meetings, "She's seen and heard it all....She asks you well-informed and brilliant questions that make you think about the things you're doing."

The Queen greets Marilyn Monroe at the Royal Film Performance in London's Leicester Square ahead of the screening of the film *The Battle of the River Plate*. They were both 30 years old. This was their only meeting. Monroe died six years later.

OCTOBER 27, 1958

Singer Frank Sinatra bows his head as he is introduced to the Queen at the premiere of the film *Me and the Colonel* in London. Buckingham Palace says there are "no obligatory codes of behavior" when meeting the royal family, but many people do choose to observe a traditional greeting. For men, this is a bow of the head; for women, a curtsy. When first presented to the Queen, the correct address is "Your Majesty"; subsequently, it's "Ma'am." For other royals, the formal address is first "Your Royal Highness" and then "Sir" or "Ma'am."

JUNE 1961

ABOVE United States President John Kennedy and First Lady Jackie Kennedy are hosted by the Queen and Prince Philip at Buckingham Palace. The visit occurred five months after the president took office. When he was assassinated two years later, in November 1963, Philip attended the state funeral in Washington, D.C. In 1965, the Queen opened a British memorial to President Kennedy at Runnymede, Surrey, saying, "The unprecedented intensity of that wave of grief, mixed with something akin to despair, which swept over our people at the news of President Kennedy's assassination, was a measure of the extent to which we recognized what he had already accomplished and of the high hopes that rode with him in a future that was not to be."

NOVEMBER 4, 1963

OPPOSITE Princess Margaret greets The Beatles after the Royal Variety Performance. The band met members of the royal family several times, including in October 1965, when they were awarded Member of the Order of the British Empire medals at Buckingham Palace. In 1997, Paul McCartney was knighted by the Queen for his service to music. Ringo Starr was also knighted, this time by Prince William, in 2018. Margaret was a working member of the royal family, supporting her sister, the Queen, in her duties. She became patron or president of more than 80 organizations, including the Royal Ballet.

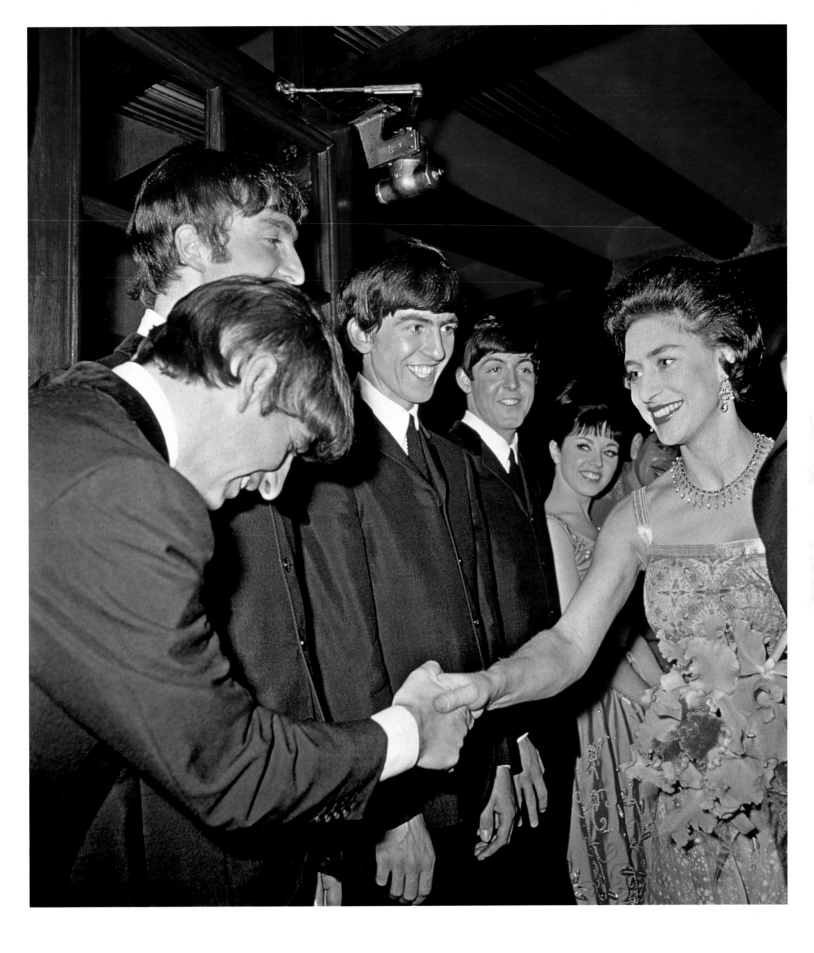

OCTOBER 14, 1969

Apollo 11 astronauts Michael Collins, Neil Armstrong, and Buzz Aldrin (left to right) meet the Queen at Buckingham Palace. Elizabeth hosted the crew a few months after their historic July moon landing. Like other heads of state, she sent a message that was carried on the mission: "On behalf of the British people, I salute the skills and courage which have brought man to the moon. May this endeavor increase the knowledge and well-being of mankind."

FEBRUARY 1972

The Queen is met with a guard of honor during her journey to Thailand. She was hosted by Thai King Bhumibol and Queen Sirikit during the six-day state visit and accompanied by Prince Philip and Princess Anne. King Bhumibol died in 2016, after having reigned for 70 years and 126 days. On his death, Queen Elizabeth assumed the record as the world's longest-reigning living monarch. However, the world's longest-reigning monarch ever is Louis XIV, the king of France who reigned for 72 years and 110 days.

MARCH 17, 1975

The Queen shakes hands with actress Barbra Streisand before the Royal Film Performance of *Funny Lady*, in which Streisand stars. A cheer went up from the crowds assembled in London's Leicester Square when the Queen arrived for the event.

NOVEMBER 10, 1975

The Queen greets members of the KwaZulu Dance Company following the Royal Variety Performance at the London Palladium. The annual theater event is attended by members of the royal family and raises money for the Royal Variety Charity to support those who have worked in the entertainment industry. The Queen has been patron of the charity since the start of her reign.

JULY 7, 1976

The Queen dances with President Gerald Ford during a dinner in her honor at the White House. The Queen and Prince Philip have made five visits to the United States since she became monarch: in 1957, 1976 (for the Bicentennial), 1983, 1991, and 2007. In her Christmas broadcast in 1976, the Queen said, "Who would have thought 200 years ago that a descendant of King George III could have taken part in these celebrations?...The United States was born in bitter conflict with Britain, but we didn't remain enemies for long."

MAY 28, 1982

The Queen and Pope John Paul II walk through Buckingham Palace during his historic visit to the United Kingdom. John Paul II became the first reigning pope to visit the United Kingdom in 1982, touring nine cities and delivering several addresses. The trip was almost canceled because of the Falklands war but went ahead with an agreement that the pope would not meet Prime Minister Margaret Thatcher.

FEBRUARY 27, 1983

Singers Perry Como, Frank Sinatra, and Dionne Warwick meet the Queen during her visit to California. They entertained her at a banquet given in Elizabeth's honor by the city of Los Angeles. While on the trip, she also visited Yosemite National Park.

The Queen presents Mother Teresa with the Order of Merit during a visit to India. The award is a personal one from the Queen to people with outstanding ability and accomplishment. Mother Teresa received it in recognition of her service to humanity during a presentation at the Presidential Palace in New Delhi.

JULY 9, 1996

The Queen rides in a carriage with President Nelson Mandela along the Mall during his state visit to the United Kingdom, one of several occasions they met. In her memoir *Good Morning, Mr. Mandela*, former Mandela assistant Zelda la Grange said that the South African leader and the Queen enjoyed a "warm friendship." She wrote, "'Oh, Elizabeth,' he would say when he greeted her, and she would respond, 'Hello, Nelson.' I think he was one of the very few people who called her by her first name, and she seemed to be amused by it."

JUNE 24, 2003

President Vladimir Putin, of Russia, and the Queen as she disembarks from a carriage during his state visit to the United Kingdom. His visit was the first by a Russian leader to the United Kingdom in more than 125 years and took place against the backdrop of human rights protests. The Queen has hosted many controversial leaders, yet her role is purely ceremonial and she has no say in whom she meets on such occasions, whether at home or abroad. Those decisions are made by the British government.

JUNE 24, 2010

The Queen shares a laugh with tennis stars Roger Federer, Serena Williams, and Novak Djokovic (left to right) during the Wimbledon lawn tennis tournament. The Queen was patron of the All England Lawn Tennis and Croquet Club, which hosts the tournament, from 1952 until 2016, when Elizabeth passed the role to the Duchess of Cambridge.

MAY 25, 2011

The Queen joins President Barack Obama and First Lady Michelle Obama ahead of a dinner at the residence of the United States ambassador to the United Kingdom during the president's state visit. The Queen hosted the Obamas for the three-day visit, and the couple stayed at Buckingham Palace. She hosted them again in 2016 during a less formal trip when they had lunch with her and Prince Philip at Windsor Castle.

JUNE 4, 2012

The Queen shakes hands with musician Elton John at the concert to celebrate her Diamond Jubilee as singers Cliff Richard, Shirley Bassey, and Tom Jones (left to right) wait to greet her. The concert on the Mall in front of Buckingham Palace saw a star-studded lineup of musicians perform for the royal family and the 10,000 members of the public who won free tickets in a national ballot, alongside 2,000 people from charities associated with the royal family.

OCTOBER 18, 2013

The Queen meets Pakistani schoolgirl Malala Yousafzai. Malala became a worldwide hero after surviving an assassination attempt by the Taliban, who shot her in the head when she was 15 for campaigning for girls to have the right to go to school. She was flown to the United Kingdom for treatment and has since addressed the United Nations and won the Nobel Peace Prize, at age 17—the youngest person to do so. Malala presented the Queen with a copy of her book *I Am Malala* at a reception for Commonwealth, youth, and education at Buckingham Palace.

FEBRUARY 17, 2014

Dame Helen Mirren stands before the Queen during a Buckingham Palace reception for the dramatic arts. The actress won an Oscar for her starring role in the 2006 film *The Queen*. After her meeting with the Queen, Mirren told reporters, "I am genuinely always astounded by her aura, her twinkle, her presence. It never fails to surprise me, and again, it's what everyone says when they meet her—it was what overwhelmed me the first time I met her." Mirren had been made a dame in 2003 for services to the performing arts.

The Queen and Pope Francis exchange gifts during her visit to the Vatican. For the first time when visiting the Vatican, the Queen did not wear black but instead chose a lilac-colored coat and matching hat. It was suggested by commentators that this demonstrated a more relaxed and progressive outlook on the part of the Vatican. The meeting was originally scheduled for March 2013, but it was postponed after the Queen was briefly admitted to the hospital with symptoms of gastroenteritis.

The Queen speaks with Professor Stephen Hawking at a St. James's Palace reception for the charity Leonard Cheshire, which provides support for people with disabilities. The Queen has met with Hawking several times. Following this encounter, his nurse Patricia O'Dowd told reporters, "The Queen said, 'Have you still got that American voice?' Stephen said, 'Yes, it is copyrighted, actually.'"

OCTOBER 10, 2014

The Queen greets actress and humanitarian Angelina Jolie during a private audience at Buckingham Palace. Jolie was made an honorary dame for her work campaigning against sexual violence in war.

JULY 17, 2020

The Queen knights Captain Tom Moore during a special investiture ceremony on the grounds of Windsor Castle, when she presented him with the insignia of the Knight Bachelor. During the onset of the 2020 coronavirus pandemic, Captain Tom became an international hero for his incredible fundraising efforts for the National Health Service. Originally setting out to raise £1,000 for NHS charities by walking laps around his garden, he ended up raising more than £32 million by the time he turned 100. The unique ceremony was carried out despite the fact that investitures were postponed during the pandemic.

Sovereign of Style

—·—

"YOUR MAJESTY, I KNOW THAT YOU DO NOT WISH TO BE KNOWN AS A FASHION ICON, BUT FOR ALL OF US IN THIS ROOM, WHO HAVE THE UTMOST RESPECT FOR YOU, AND ALSO FOR THE HARD WORK, DILIGENCE, AND CULTURAL IMPACT ON OUR INDUSTRY, WE KNOW THAT YOU UNDOUBTEDLY ARE."

— Caroline Rush, chief executive of the British Fashion Council, in a speech during the Queen's appearance at London Fashion Week, February 20, 2018

JUNE 14, 2012

The Queen wears a lilac coat by Stewart Parvin and a matching hat by Rachel Trevor-Morgan during a day trip to Hertfordshire, England, in her Diamond Jubilee year.

The Queen's fashion choices form an integral part of her identity—from her dresses and coats in bright block colors that make her easy to spot in a crowd to her intricate evening gowns for the most glittering formal occasions. Those who have seen her in person often comment on the fact that she is small in stature. Yet the Queen is instantly recognizable thanks to her consistent and timeless style.

Elizabeth can most often be found in a colorful matching dress and hat, white gloves, and sensible black leather shoes while clutching her black Launer handbag. "She needs to stand out for people to be able to say, 'I saw the Queen,'" said Sophie, the Countess of Wessex, in the ITV documentary *Our Queen at Ninety*. "Don't forget," she added, "that when she turns up somewhere, the crowds are two, three, four, 10, 15 deep, and someone wants to be able to say they saw a bit of the Queen's hat as she went past." Elizabeth is also the master of diplomatic dressing, carefully choosing her outfits, through color and motif, to pay tribute to her hosts or guests and always respecting local customs and traditions. From her selection of yellow when she visits Australia to, memorably, green for her historic visit to the Republic of Ireland, the Queen's sartorial choices can play a key part in her diplomatic work.

In the early years of her reign, the Queen called on designers Norman Hartnell and Hardy Amies to create the statement pieces in her wardrobe. Today, she relies on her designer, personal assistant, and senior dresser, Angela Kelly, one of her most trusted aides. The Queen also frequently wears designs by Stewart Parvin and milliner Rachel Trevor-Morgan. In a 2007 interview with the *Sunday Telegraph*, Kelly said of her relationship with the Queen, "We are two typical women. We discuss clothes, makeup, jewelry. We say, 'Would this piece of jewelry look nice with that outfit?' and things like that."

Elizabeth consistently champions the British fashion industry, and those who supply goods or services to the Queen could be awarded with a coveted Royal Warrant. However, her first appearance at London Fashion Week was not until 2018, when she sat in the front row. At the event, the Queen presented the inaugural Queen Elizabeth II Award for British Design and said in a speech, "From the tweed of the Hebrides to Nottingham lace and, of course, Carnaby Street, our fashion industry has been renowned for outstanding craftsmanship for many years and continues to produce world-class textiles and cutting-edge, practical designs."

NOVEMBER 20, 1947

Princess Elizabeth and Philip Mountbatten depart Westminster Abbey on their wedding day. Her dress, by Norman Hartnell, was approved less than three months before the event. According to the royal household, he cited Botticelli's painting *Primavera*, symbolizing the coming of spring, as inspiration for the design. Due to World War II rationing measures still in place, Elizabeth used clothing coupons to pay for the dress material, with the British government allowing her 200 extra coupons. It was made from ivory silk with flower motifs and decorated with crystals and 10,000 seed pearls imported from the United States. The gown had a 15-foot silk tulle full court train embroidered with pearls and crystals. It was later exhibited at St. James's Palace before going on tour across the United Kingdom.

JUNE 2, 1953

The Queen appears in her coronation dress, also designed by Norman Hartnell. The dress has been described by the Royal Collection Trust as "one of the most important examples of 20th-century design." It was made of white satin and embroidered with the emblems of the United Kingdom and Commonwealth in gold and silver thread. Since her coronation, the Queen has worn the dress a handful of times, including to open Parliament in New Zealand and Australia in 1954.

Hats Off for Headscarves

A headscarf is one of the Queen's favorite accessories. When dressing informally, Elizabeth is most often seen with a brightly colored silk headscarf tied under her chin. Her headscarf label of choice is Hermès, the French fashion house, and she has shown off a huge collection throughout the years. She wore a headscarf at the 1956 Olympic Games equestrian events in Stockholm, Sweden, as shown here with her sister, Princess Margaret (top). She often sports one during the annual Royal Windsor Horse Show (left) and even wore a headscarf to greet United States President Barack Obama and First Lady Michelle Obama when they visited for lunch at Windsor Castle in 2016 (above).

A Hat for Every Occasion

Hats are a very important feature of the Queen's wardrobe and she has often worn them to make a statement. In a 2007 letter to milliner Philip Somerville, the Queen thanked him for making her hats and wrote that she "must be almost the only person who wears hats constantly!" In 2018, milliner Philip Treacy, whose hats are frequently worn by members of the royal family (as above, top right in black and white and in yellow), told BBC Radio 4, "Her Majesty the Queen has kept hats alive in the imagination of people all over the world."

The Queen's Handbag

The Queen with her trusty Launer handbag. She is rarely seen without one, and there is much speculation about what she carries inside. "She favors black, black patent, cream, and, on occasion, gold," said Launer CEO Gerald Bodmer about the Queen's choice of color. Each Launer bag is handcrafted using the finest leather. On several occasions, the Queen has been seen applying a lipstick she has taken from her handbag. A compact mirror is also thought to be a staple, along with tissues, reading glasses, a pen, and mints. The Queen rarely carries money but is thought to take some to church on Sundays to leave a donation. She has also been rumored to use her handbag to give signals to her staff, although this has never been confirmed officially. It has been said that if she puts her handbag on the table, it signifies she is ready to leave an event, and if she puts it on the floor, it means she is tired of the conversation.

1975

ABOVE The Queen wears white gloves during a state visit to Mexico. She always wears gloves on formal occasions and is supplied by Cornelia James. The label is an eponym for its founder, who first made gloves for Elizabeth for her going-away outfit on her wedding day. The Queen most often wears white gloves, but she also has black and ivory pairs.

AUGUST 22, 1972

ABOVE The Queen, Prince Philip, and their four children stand in front of Balmoral Castle. The Queen wears the Balmoral tartan, designed by Queen Victoria's husband, Prince Albert, in 1853. The Queen and her personal piper are the only ones currently approved to wear this tartan. Members of the royal family can wear it only with her permission. The royal family often wears tartan when in Scotland, with male family members frequently appearing in kilts, such as Prince Charles shown here.

JUNE 16, 1979

RIGHT The Queen wears a military uniform for her annual official birthday parade, Trooping the Colour. In the earlier years of her reign, she rode on horseback and wore a military dress uniform designed by equestrian tailor Bernard Weatherill and hats by couture milliner Aage Thaarup.

The Queen wears a floor-length black dress and a veil during her visit to the Vatican to meet with Pope John Paul II. She also chose the Vladimir Tiara with pearls for the occasion. It is unusual to see the Queen in black, except during mourning. However, she respects local traditions when on official visits. This was her third visit to the Vatican and her second as queen.

FEBRUARY 28, 1983

The Queen and Nancy Reagan, the First Lady of the United States, arrive for a concert in Santa Barbara during the Queen's visit to California. Elizabeth's dress, designed by Hardy Amies, was embroidered with California poppies as a tribute to her hosts. This sartorial demonstration of appreciation, especially on official visits, is one the Queen has employed on many occasions, and it has also been adopted by other members of the royal family. For example, when the Duchess of Cambridge visited New Zealand in 2014, she wore a dress embroidered with the country's unofficial national emblem, the silver fern.

DECEMBER 29, 1985

The Queen wears a fur coat during an outing with grandson Peter Phillips during the holidays at Sandringham, in the English county of Norfolk. Elizabeth has worn fur throughout her reign and has been criticized for this by animal rights activists. Her dresser, Angela Kelly, wrote in her 2019 book, *The Other Side of the Coin: The Queen, the Dresser, and the Wardrobe*, that going forward, fake fur would be used. This new approach was praised; however, it was noted that the Queen would still wear existing items in her wardrobe made from animal fur.

The Queen arrives at Ascot Racecourse in Berkshire in the traditional carriage procession for Royal Ascot, the world-famous annual race meeting. She stands out in her bright-blue outfit and hat. Betting on the color of the Queen's hat is a popular activity during Royal Ascot. The Queen's dresser, Angela Kelly, shared in her book *The Other Side of the Coin* that ahead of the event, she lays out a number of decoy hats to "stop anyone catching sight of the hat Her Majesty actually intends to wear and, with inside knowledge, betting a vast amount of money on the correct color of the Queen's hat."

MAY 14, 1991

ABOVE The Queen delivers a speech on the lawn of the White House as United States President George H. W. Bush listens. The Queen, partially hidden behind the tall podium, was described as a "talking hat." Her speech was broadcast around the world, and yet her face could barely be seen. Later in the visit, the Queen made a historic address to Congress and drew laughter and a standing ovation when she quipped, "I do hope you can see me today from where you are."

OCTOBER 2004

RIGHT A rare photograph of the Queen without shoes as she visits the Gurdwara Sri Guru Singh Sabha, a large Sikh temple in West London. The Queen removed her shoes to tour the temple in stockinged feet.

AUGUST 2, 2010

The Queen wears trousers as she disembarks the cruise ship *Hebridean Princess* in Scrabster, on the north coast of Scotland. She had been on a family holiday to mark Princess Anne's 60th birthday. The Queen is almost never seen in trousers while on duty; however, she has been photographed in them a handful of times when not working. When she is at the annual Royal Windsor Horse Show or out riding, she has also been photographed wearing jodhpurs.

MAY 18, 2011

The Queen makes a speech during a state banquet at Dublin Castle on her historic visit to Ireland. In addition to her words, her outfit also helped send a powerful message of respect to the host nation. Designed by Angela Kelly, the white dress featured a bodice with 2,091 hand-sewn silk shamrocks. An Irish harp brooch, made of crystals, was pinned to the Queen's shoulder.

JUNE 5, 2014

The Queen wears patent leather shoes during an official visit to Paris. She almost always wears black leather shoes with a low heel made by Covent Garden shoemaker Anello & Davide so she can be comfortable on her feet during long days. Although she is supplied with new pairs, she also has her current shoes repaired. Her dressmaker Stewart Parvin told the *Sunday Times* in 2012 that she has someone else break in her new pairs of shoes: "The Queen can never say, 'I'm uncomfortable; I can't walk anymore.' She has the right to have someone wear them in." In her 2019 book about dressing the Queen, Angela Kelly revealed, "A flunky wears in Her Majesty's shoes to ensure that they are comfortable and that she is always good to go. And, yes, I am that flunky."

APRIL 1, 2011

The Queen holds on to her hat as she arrives at Royal Air Force Valley, on the Isle of Anglesey, in Wales. It can be difficult to predict a sudden gust of wind, but the Queen's outfits are carefully planned with the weather in mind. In her 2012 book, *Dressing the Queen: The Jubilee Wardrobe*, Angela Kelly wrote, "The Queen undertakes a wide range of engagements, many of which take place in the open air, where a sudden breeze could cause embarrassment. If we think this is a possibility, we will very occasionally use weights, discreetly sewn into the seams of day dresses."

JULY 17, 2014

ABOVE Standing out in her bright blue against a sea of orange, the Queen poses for a photograph with construction workers during her visit to open the Reading railway station. During daytime visits, the Queen most often wears a bright matching dress and hat.

JUNE 11, 2016

RIGHT The royal family appears on the balcony of Buckingham Palace for the annual Trooping the Colour ceremony during the Queen's 90th birthday year. Elizabeth's bright-green outfit, designed by Stewart Parvin, generated much excitement on social media, inspiring the hashtag #NeonAt90.

DECEMBER 8, 2016

Senior members of the royal family gather for the annual Buckingham Palace reception for members of the diplomatic corps based in the United Kingdom. This white-tie event is the most formal one in the royal calendar. For this occasion, the Queen most often chooses white, which acts as a backdrop for the blue sash and other colorful adornments she wears in her capacity as Sovereign of the Order of the Garter. From left, the Duchess of Cornwall, Prince Charles, the Queen, Prince Philip, and the Duke and Duchess of Cambridge.

Royal Repeats

The Queen wears the same outfit on four different occasions between 2003 and 2007. This fuchsia-pink ensemble with a purple hat has been a favorite of the Queen's. She often wears her outfits multiple times and has items mended rather than replaced.

FEBRUARY 20, 2018

The Queen observes a show during London Fashion Week with Vogue editor in chief Dame Anna Wintour (second from right) and Angela Kelly (far right). Kelly's formal title is Her Majesty's Personal Adviser and Curator (The Queen's Jewellery, Insignias, and Wardrobe), Senior Dresser, and In-House Designer. However, she is often described as the Queen's gatekeeper because of her uniquely close bond with the monarch. Kelly began working for the royal household in 1994 after the Queen met her during an official visit to Germany and was impressed with her discretion. In 2007, Kelly told the *Sunday Telegraph*, "I don't know why the Queen seems fond of me—because I don't give her an easy time! I do think she values my opinion, but she is the one who is in control." Kelly has designed many of the Queen's most iconic outfits and was given rare permission to write two books about dressing the monarch, published in 2012 and 2019.

An Umbrella for Every Outfit

The Queen, the Queen Mother, Princess Margaret, the Duke and Duchess of Cambridge, Prince Harry, and the Duchess of Cornwall shelter from the rain with umbrellas. When the weather is wet, the Queen most often turns to an umbrella designed by Fulton Umbrellas, the United Kingdom manufacturer. Its Birdcage umbrellas first became popular with the Queen Mother, who thought the clear, domed cover would offer protection while allowing her to remain visible.

The Queen wears a blue hat dotted with blue-and-yellow flowers to the state opening of Parliament. As she made her speech outlining the government's plans as the United Kingdom prepared to leave the European Union, several people compared her hat to its flag. The European Parliament's chief Brexit negotiator, Guy Verhofstadt, even posted on social media: "Clearly the EU still inspires some in the U.K." Often there is symbolism in the Queen's outfits; however, on this occasion, her dresser, Angela Kelly, later pointed out that the similarity noted was not intentional. Kelly wrote in her 2019 book, "It was a coincidence, but boy, did it attract a lot of attention, and it certainly made us smile."

CHAPTER SEVEN

All That Glitters

"SO THERE ARE SOME DISADVANTAGES TO CROWNS, BUT OTHERWISE, THEY'RE QUITE IMPORTANT THINGS."

—The Queen, during the BBC documentary *The Coronation*, January 2018

JUNE 2, 1953

The Queen arrives at Westminster Abbey for her coronation wearing her coronation dress and the Diamond Diadem, also known as the George IV State Diadem.

When we think of the monarchy, one of the first things that springs to mind is royal regalia—from the Crown Jewels used at coronations to the Queen's glittering personal collection of tiaras, earrings, necklaces, and brooches.

The priceless Crown Jewels are powerful symbols of the British monarchy and considered to be the most complete collection of royal regalia in the world. Comprising crowns, robes, swords, scepters, and other items, the Crown Jewels are kept under armed guard in the Tower of London, where they can be viewed by tourists except on the few occasions when they are in use. The Crown Jewels are not owned by the monarch personally but rather part of the Royal Collection kept in trust for her successors and the nation. The approximately 140 ceremonial objects on display are adorned with 23,578 gemstones, including stones cut from the magnificent Cullinan Diamond—the largest diamond ever found. The centerpiece of the collection is the St. Edward's Crown, which was made for the coronation of Charles II in 1661 and used to crown the Queen on her own coronation day. Also on display at the Tower of London is the Imperial State Crown worn by the Queen at the end of the coronation ceremony when she left Westminster Abbey. She also wears it for the annual state opening of Parliament.

While the Crown Jewels are worn rarely, the Queen regularly showcases pieces from her extensive personal collection of jewels and loans them to members of her family for special occasions. She has worn tiaras on so many occasions—from state banquets to white-tie diplomatic receptions—that Princess Margaret is understood to have said, "The Queen is the only person who can put on a tiara with one hand while walking down the stairs." The Queen's dresser, Angela Kelly, revealed in her 2019 book, *The Other Side of the Coin*, that gin and water are used to give royal diamonds "extra sparkle."

Many of the pieces in the Queen's personal collection have been handed down through generations of royalty or presented to her on special occasions. The Queen often uses her jewelry to pay tribute to guests or hosts, much as she does with her choice of dress. In 1954, the Queen received the Wattle Brooch from the people of Australia and has worn it during visits to the country since. On visits to Canada, she has often chosen the Maple Leaf Brooch, which was given to her mother by her father to mark their 1939 tour of Canada.

THE CROWN JEWELS

The Crown Jewels on display in the Tower of London. The original collection was destroyed under the orders of Oliver Cromwell following the execution of King Charles I in 1649. Cromwell served as Lord Protector of England, Scotland, and Ireland during a brief period when the monarchy was abolished. Under his rule, the gemstones were removed from the Crown Jewels and their precious metals melted to make coins. One item to survive was the 12th-century coronation spoon. After the monarchy was restored in 1660, a new set of Crown Jewels (right) was made for Charles II's coronation in 1661. They were guarded at the Tower of London by Yeomen Warders, or Beefeaters. Today, the Beefeaters comprise men and women retired from the Armed Forces who conduct tours and work alongside the tower guard to protect the Crown Jewels. No one is sure of the origin of the name Beefeaters, but a popular theory is that they could eat as much as they wanted from the sovereign's table. In addition to crowns, the tower collection includes swords, trumpets, maces, orbs, rings, scepters, and an ampulla to hold the consecrated oil for the anointing of a monarch. During World War II, gemstones from the Crown Jewels were hidden in a biscuit tin at Windsor Castle.

The St. Edward's Crown

Described by Historic Royal Palaces as "the most important and sacred of all the crowns," the St. Edward's Crown is used only for the moment of crowning itself. During Queen Elizabeth II's coronation ceremony, she sat in the King Edward's Chair, which was made around 1300. The Archbishop of Canterbury then placed the St. Edward's Crown on her head. It weighs 4 pounds, 12 ounces, and the solid-gold frame is set with 444 stones, including rubies, amethysts, sapphires, garnet, topaz, and tourmalines. The crown has a purple velvet cap with an ermine band. During the ceremony, the coronation ring was placed on the fourth finger of the Queen's right hand as a symbol of dignity. The ring, known as the Sovereign's Ring, was made for the coronation of William IV, in 1831. It features a sapphire overlaid with rubies in the shape of a cross and surrounded by diamonds.

MAY 12, 1937

The Queen Mother, then Queen Elizabeth, with Princess Elizabeth on the Buckingham Palace balcony following the coronation of her husband, King George VI.

Queen Elizabeth the Queen Mother's Crown

This crown was made specially for the Queen Mother for the 1937 coronation. She later wore it to her daughter's coronation in 1953, and it was placed on her coffin during her funeral procession in 2002. The large diamond on the front is the Koh-i-Noor, meaning "Mountain of Light," one of the most famous gems in the world. The diamond was presented to Queen Victoria in 1850, but its ownership is a much-contested subject. Where exactly it was found has not been confirmed, but by 1849, it was in the possession of the 10-year-old ruler of the Punjab, Maharaja Duleep Singh. He signed over his kingdom and the diamond to the British East India Company, which seized control of large parts of the Indian subcontinent. In 2009, Tushar Gandhi, the great-grandson of Indian Independence leader Mahatma Gandhi, told *The Times* that the diamond "rightfully" belonged to India and returning it would "be atonement for the colonial past." Claims have been made from both India and Pakistan for the gem to be returned, as the Punjab was divided between them when the region gained independence from Britain in 1947.

Sovereign's Orb and Jewelled Sword of Offering

During the coronation ceremony, the sovereign is presented with the Sovereign's Orb (left) and Jewelled Sword of Offering. The Orb is a hollow gold sphere decorated with pearls, diamonds, rubies, emeralds, sapphires, and amethyst. It is placed in the monarch's right hand before being settled on the altar and symbolizes the Christian world. The Jewelled Sword of Offering is presented to the new monarch as part of a collection of regalia that represents chivalry. It is set with stones including diamonds, emeralds, and rubies and decorated with the national emblems of England, Scotland, and Ireland: roses, thistles, and shamrocks.

JUNE 2, 1953

ABOVE The Queen hands the Jewelled Sword of Offering to the Dean of Westminster before being crowned.

Sovereign's Sceptre with Cross and Sovereign's Sceptre with Dove

Before being crowned, the sovereign is presented with two scepters, one in each hand. The Sovereign's Sceptre with Cross (left) represents the monarch's temporal power. It contains the Cullinan I Diamond, the world's largest colorless cut diamond, weighing 530.2 carats. This was the largest stone cut from the Cullinan Diamond, which was found in January 1905 in a mine near Pretoria, South Africa. The gem was presented to King Edward VII in 1907 and later cut into nine stones. Edward's successor, King George V, had Cullinan I, also known as the Star of Africa, mounted in the Sovereign's Sceptre with Cross in 1910. The Sovereign's Sceptre with Dove, also known as the Rod of Equity and Mercy, symbolizes the sovereign's spiritual role. It is made of a plain gold rod and topped with an enamel dove with outspread wings representing the Holy Ghost.

JUNE 2, 1953

ABOVE The Queen after she has been crowned during her coronation ceremony. She is wearing the St. Edward's Crown and holding the Sovereign's Sceptre with Cross in her right hand and the Sovereign's Sceptre with Dove in her left hand.

The Queen wears the Imperial State Crown following her
coronation ceremony. She is carrying the Sovereign's Orb and
Sovereign's Sceptre with Cross.

The Imperial State Crown

The Imperial State Crown is worn by sovereigns at the end of the coronation ceremony, replacing the St. Edward's Crown. It is also worn at the state opening of Parliament. One of the most elaborate pieces of regalia, it is set with 2,868 diamonds and other stones, including 17 sapphires, 11 emeralds, and 269 pearls. At the front of the crown is Cullinan II, the second largest stone cut from the Cullinan Diamond. The Queen has not worn the 2-pound, 5-ounce crown for the state opening of Parliament since 2016 due to its heavy weight and her advancing years. In 2019, the crown was placed on a cushion next to her instead.

NOVEMBER 23, 2004

ABOVE The Queen wears the Imperial State Crown at the state opening of Parliament.

RIGHT The Imperial State Crown.

THE QUEEN'S PERSONAL JEWELRY COLLECTION

Diamond Diadem

NOVEMBER 15, 2006

The Queen arrives for the state opening of
Parliament wearing the Diamond Diadem Tiara.
This tiara was made for King George IV's coronation,
in 1821, and is set with 1,333 diamonds. This is the
crown that the Queen wore when traveling to her
coronation and that she still wears when arriving
for the state opening of Parliament. It is a familiar
sight on stamps and coins and contains emblems
of England (roses), Scotland (thistles), and Ireland
(shamrocks). During the 2019 state opening of
Parliament, the Queen chose to wear the Diamond
Diadem Tiara for her speech instead of switching to
the much heavier Imperial State Crown.

Wedding Jewelry

JULY 10, 1947

Newly engaged Princess Elizabeth and Philip Mountbatten pose for a photograph at Buckingham Palace. Philip had a platinum-and-diamond engagement ring made for Elizabeth using diamonds from a tiara belonging to his mother, Princess Alice of Battenberg. His wedding present to his wife was a bracelet made from the same tiara. On her wedding day, Elizabeth wore Queen Mary's Fringe Tiara, which was made in 1919 for her grandmother. On the morning of the wedding, the tiara snapped when it was being fitted into her hair and had to be repaired. In the photographs, you can see a slight gap between the central spoke and the one to its right. Elizabeth also wore diamond-and-pearl earrings along with a double-strand pearl necklace made from two necklaces that had been in the royal family for centuries. Elizabeth's wedding ring was made of Welsh gold—a tradition since her parents' wedding in 1923, when the royal family was given a nugget. Subsequent royal wedding rings, including those of Princess Diana, the Duchess of Cambridge, and the Duchess of Sussex, have also been made from Welsh gold.

NOVEMBER 20, 1947

TOP Princess Elizabeth smiles on her wedding day.

NOVEMBER 14, 1973

MIDDLE Princess Anne wears Queen Mary's Fringe Tiara for her wedding to Captain Mark Phillips.

JULY 17, 2020

RIGHT Princess Beatrice wears Queen Mary's Fringe Tiara for her wedding to Edoardo Mapelli Mozzi.

The Greville Bequest

In 1942, society hostess Dame Margaret Greville left her extensive precious jewelry collection to the Queen Mother. It is still not known exactly how many pieces the black tin box of treasures contained, but the collection remains popular with the royal family today. One of the standout pieces is the Greville Tiara, a favorite with the Queen Mother and now frequently worn by the Duchess of Cornwall. It is sometimes referred to as the Boucheron Honeycomb Tiara because of its pattern and the fact that it was made by Boucheron, the Parisian jeweler. Jewelry given to Princess Elizabeth as wedding presents included the platinum-and-diamond Greville Chandelier Earrings and the Ruby and Diamond Floral Bandeau Necklace. She was also given a set of two Greville Ivy Leaf Brooches for her 21st birthday. Princess Eugenie borrowed the Greville Emerald Kokoshnik Tiara for her wedding to Jack Brooksbank, in October 2018.

OCTOBER 12, 1951

LEFT Princess Elizabeth wears the Ruby and Diamond Floral Bandeau Necklace at a banquet in Ottawa, Ontario, Canada.

NOVEMBER 4, 1958

ABOVE The Queen wears a Greville Ivy Leaf Brooch on her hatband.

NOVEMBER 23, 2007

LEFT The Duchess of Cornwall attends a banquet in Uganda in the Greville Tiara.

OCTOBER 12, 2018

BELOW Princess Eugenie wears the Greville Emerald Kokoshnik Tiara on her wedding day.

NOVEMBER 19, 1964

ABOVE The Queen Mother wears the Greville Tiara and Greville Peardrop Earrings.

DECEMBER 2017

RIGHT The Duchess of Cambridge appears for the Spanish state banquet in the Ruby and Diamond Floral Bandeau Necklace.

TIARAS

Vladimir Tiara

The diamond-and-pearl Vladimir Tiara was originally made in 1874 for Grand Duchess Maria Pavlovna, wife of Grand Duke Vladimir of the Romanov dynasty, at the time of her marriage. The Grand Duchess Vladimir had a renowned collection, which was smuggled out of Russia during the Russian Revolution. The tiara was purchased by Queen Mary in 1921 after the grand duchess's death. It can be worn different ways by exchanging the pearls with emeralds or by removing the stones altogether.

APRIL 29, 1980

TOP The Queen chooses the Vladimir Tiara paired with Queen Victoria's Golden Jubilee Necklace for a banquet during a visit to Switzerland.

2015

RIGHT The Queen wears the emerald-encrusted Vladimir Tiara and the Delhi Durbar Necklace for a dinner during the Commonwealth Heads of Government Meeting in Malta.

Queen Alexandra's Kokoshnik Tiara

NOVEMBER 1967

The Queen dances with Prince Philip wearing Queen Alexandra's Kokoshnik Tiara during a visit to Malta. The Kokoshnik Tiara was presented to Queen Alexandra, the wife of King Edward VII, when she was the Princess of Wales, for her 25th wedding anniversary in 1888. On Alexandra's death in 1925, it was passed down to her daughter-in-law Queen Mary and then to the Queen. Inspired by a traditional Russian headdress, it is made of 61 diamond bars and can also be worn as a necklace.

Girls of Great Britain and Ireland Tiara

DECEMBER 12, 1967

Smiling broadly, the Queen dazzles in winter white as she arrives at a film premiere wearing the Girls of Great Britain and Ireland Tiara. This is one of the most recognizable tiaras in her personal collection, and she has been depicted wearing it on certain issues of British and Commonwealth banknotes and coins. The tiara was a gift to Queen Mary on her wedding day in July 1893, and she gave it to her granddaughter Princess Elizabeth as a wedding present in 1947. Angela Kelly, the Queen's dresser, described in her 2012 book how Elizabeth is "very fond" of the tiara, which she has worn often throughout her reign.

Queen Mary's Lover's Knot Tiara

Made for Queen Mary and inherited by the Queen, this tiara was worn many times by Princess Diana after her wedding in 1981. After Diana's divorce from Prince Charles in 1996, the tiara was returned to the royal family. Today, the tiara is frequently worn by the Duchess of Cambridge for state banquets and the Queen's annual diplomatic reception.

APRIL 1955

ABOVE Wearing Queen Mary's Lover's Knot Tiara, the Queen arrives for a dinner to mark the retirement of Prime Minister Winston Churchill.

APRIL 29, 1983

ABOVE Princess Diana wears the diamond-and-pearl Lover's Knot Tiara during a banquet in Auckland, New Zealand.

DECEMBER 4, 2018

LEFT The Duchess of Cambridge greets guests wearing Queen Mary's Lover's Knot Tiara at a reception for members of the diplomatic corps.

Oriental Circlet Tiara

NOVEMBER 23, 2005

The Queen wears the Oriental Circlet Tiara with the Baring Ruby Necklace during a state visit to Malta. This is the only time she has worn this tiara, which was a favorite of her mother's. The piece was originally designed by Prince Albert for Queen Victoria and was later altered by Queen Alexandra, who replaced the opals with rubies.

Burmese Ruby Tiara

JUNE 3, 2019

The Queen wears the Burmese Ruby Tiara and the Crown Ruby Necklace during United States President Donald Trump's state visit to the United Kingdom. This tiara was made by the House of Garrard in 1973 with diamonds from the Nizam of Hyderabad Tiara and 96 rubies that were given to her as a wedding present from the people of Burma (now Myanmar).

Cartier Halo Tiara

APRIL 29, 2011

Kate Middleton wears a tiara and a veil on her
wedding day. The Queen loaned Kate the Cartier
Halo Tiara, also known as the Scroll Tiara, for her
wedding. The tiara was originally commissioned by
King George VI for his wife, and the Queen Mother
gave it to Princess Elizabeth on her 18th birthday.
It is set with 739 brilliant and 149 baton diamonds.

OCTOBER 1954

Princess Margaret wears the Cartier Halo Tiara for
a state banquet at Buckingham Palace in honor of
the Emperor of Ethiopia, Haile Selassie.

Queen Mary's Bandeau Tiara

MAY 19, 2018

Meghan Markle waves to the crowd in Queen Mary's Bandeau Tiara on her wedding day. The diamond-and-platinum bandeau was made in 1932 for Queen Mary, incorporating a detachable brooch, which Mary already owned, at its center. The tiara was bequeathed to the Queen by Queen Mary in 1953. In an audio recording for an exhibition about their wedding outfits, Meghan said, "I was very fortunate to be able to choose this gorgeous art deco–style bandeau tiara. Harry and I had gone to Buckingham Palace to meet with Her Majesty the Queen to select one of the options that were there, which was an incredibly surreal day, as you can imagine."

BROOCHES

Flower Basket Brooch

The colorful Flower Basket Brooch was a gift from the Queen's parents to mark the birth of Prince Charles in November 1948. It has appeared on the Queen's outfits throughout the years, and she selected it to wear on Prince George's christening ceremony in 2013—65 years after she first received it.

DECEMBER 1948

Princess Elizabeth poses for an official photograph with her newborn son.

Prince Albert Brooch

FEBRUARY 1, 1977

The Queen wears the Prince Albert Brooch during an official visit to New Zealand. This sapphire-and-diamond brooch has much sentimental value for the royal family: It was a gift from Prince Albert to Queen Victoria the day before they were married, and she wore it on their wedding day, on February 10, 1840. It was handed down to her grandson's wife Queen Mary, then to the Queen Mother, and finally to the Queen.

OCTOBER 23, 2013

The Queen also wears the Flower Basket Brooch for Prince George's christening photographs, taken in the Morning Room of Clarence House. This image was the first official photograph of the Queen and her three heirs, mirroring a photograph of Queen Victoria and her three heirs taken at the christening of the future King Edward VIII in 1894.

Jardine Star Brooch

JUNE 1, 2019

ABOVE The Jardine Star Brooch sparkles on the Queen's outfit as she attends the Epsom Derby race meeting. Featuring eight diamond rays, the Victorian brooch was given to the Queen in 1981 by Lady Jardine, and she wears it frequently.

Cullinan V Brooch

MAY 11, 1980

ABOVE RIGHT A beaming Queen wears the Cullinan V Brooch during a visit to the Royal Windsor Horse Show. The heart-shaped brooch was originally worn by Queen Mary and inherited by the Queen in 1953. It is one of her favorites.

Maple Leaf Brooch

JULY 1, 2010

RIGHT The Queen wears the Maple Leaf Brooch for the Canada Day celebrations in Ottawa, Ontario. The diamond brooch was given to the Queen Mother by her husband, King George VI, in 1939 for the couple's royal tour to Canada. She loaned it to Princess Elizabeth for her first visit there, in 1951, and it was inherited by the Queen when her mother died in 2002. She has loaned the brooch to the Duchess of Cornwall and the Duchess of Cambridge for their tours of Canada.

NECKLACES

South Africa Necklace

DECEMBER 25, 1953

The young Queen wears the South Africa Necklace as she makes her Christmas broadcast from Auckland, New Zealand, during a Commonwealth tour. She was given the necklace by the people of South Africa for her 21st birthday. Elizabeth has worn it many times over the years.

Nizam of Hyderabad Necklace

JANUARY 12, 1954

The Queen wears the Nizam of Hyderabad Necklace and the Girls of Great Britain and Ireland Tiara for a portrait released during her six-month tour of the Commonwealth. The diamond-and-platinum necklace and a matching tiara were a wedding present from the Indian ruler Nizam of Hyderabad. The tiara's stones were used for the Burmese Ruby Tiara in 1973, but the necklace is still worn today. The Duchess of Cambridge borrowed it for an event at London's National Portrait Gallery in 2014 and for a diplomatic reception in 2019.

Japanese Pearl Choker

FEBRUARY 24, 1982

The Queen wears the Japanese Pearl Choker for a film premiere in London's Leicester Square. The choker was commissioned by the Queen using pearls that were a gift from the Japanese government, and she wore it frequently. She has also loaned it to Princess Diana and the Duchess of Cambridge.

NOVEMBER 1983

ABOVE The Queen attends a banquet in Hyderabad, India, wearing an aquamarine necklace and matching earrings. The set was a gift for her 1953 coronation from the president and people of Brazil.

MARCH 1996

ABOVE RIGHT The Queen dazzles in sapphires and diamonds as she attends a banquet in Prague, Czech Republic. The necklace and earrings were a wedding present from her father, King George VI, in 1947. The tiara was made in the 1960s to go with the set. The Queen also wore the necklace and earrings in an official portrait released for her Sapphire Jubilee, marking her 65 years on the throne, in 2017.

OCTOBER 2004

RIGHT The Queen wears a necklace made up of three strands of pearls for a visit to the newly refurbished Ministry of Defence Main Building, in London. The Queen is understood to have multiple necklaces in this style, including one that was a gift from her grandfather King George V for his Silver Jubilee in 1935.

A Queen's Best Friends

"THE HORSES REMAIN THE STARS, THRILLING US WITH THEIR BEAUTY, BRILLIANCE, AND COURAGE."

—The Queen, in her message in the program for Royal Ascot, June 2019

JUNE 14, 1986

The Queen rides her horse Burmese during Trooping the Colour in 1986, the last time she attended her official birthday parade on horseback. Burmese was a gift to the Queen from the Canadian Mounted Police in 1969. Elizabeth was riding Burmese during Trooping the Colour in 1981 when six blank shots were fired at her from the crowd. Marcus Sarjeant, a former air cadet, was arrested for the crime and later jailed for five years under the 1842 Treason Act.

The sight of the Queen on horseback or with corgis gathering at her feet are some of the most enduring images of her reign. Elizabeth's love of animals was fostered in childhood, when she began riding ponies and looking after the family pet dogs. Her passion for horses and dogs has formed an integral part of her public and private life.

Since being given her first corgi, Susan, when she was 18, Elizabeth has gone on to own more than 30 of the breed. She and Margaret also introduced the crossbreed dorgi to the household by mating corgis with Margaret's dachshund, Pipkin. The Queen has also kept Labradors and cocker spaniels.

The Queen's dogs are very much a part of her identity. They sit at her feet as she holds meetings with dignitaries and have been featured in official portraits and even on a Royal Mint Golden Jubilee coin. In recent years, however, she has reduced the number of dogs she has kept to two dorgis, Vulcan and Candy.

"When she's talking about her dogs or her horses, you see a completely different side to her: She relaxes," the Queen's former dog trainer Roger Mugford once told *Town & Country*. The Queen also owns and breeds racehorses. She attends race meetings Royal Ascot and Epsom Derby every year, and the sight of her cheering on the horses from the royal box is a familiar one. In 2019, it was calculated that her horses have won more than £7.7 million in prize money since 1988. It has been widely cited that her horses have won more than 1,600 races in total. Whether or not she also bets on them has not been formally revealed.

The Queen used to ride in her annual official birthday parade, Trooping the Colour. Her final appearance on horseback, on her horse Burmese, was in 1986. Since then, she has attended the ceremony in a carriage.

Elizabeth has passed on her love of horses to her children and grandchildren, with her daughter, Princess Anne, and granddaughter Zara both becoming Olympic competitors in equestrian sports. Most of the royal family are accomplished riders, with several members, including Prince Philip, Prince Charles, Prince William, and Prince Harry, playing and competing in polo as young men. Prince Philip took up carriage driving after he stopped playing polo in 1971.

In the BBC documentary *Elizabeth at 90: A Family Tribute*, Prince Charles said about his mother, "She's a marvelous rider. She's got a marvelous way with horses." The Queen has continued to ride well into her 90s and can still be spotted on her Fell pony in England's Windsor Home Park.

JULY 1936

Princess Elizabeth, at age 10, holds her corgi outside the family home at 145 Piccadilly, in London. Princesses Elizabeth and Margaret grew up with dogs after King George VI brought home Dookie, a corgi, in 1933, followed by Jane, another corgi, not long after. The sisters adored their pets.

1937

Princess Elizabeth, at age 10 or 11, rides her horse in Windsor Great Park. Elizabeth was given her first horse, a Shetland pony called Peggy, as a present from her grandfather King George V when she was four. She learned to ride as a child, and horses have remained a lifelong passion. In her book, *The Little Princesses*, former governess Marion Crawford wrote that Elizabeth and Margaret's nursery had approximately 30 toy horses in it. "The obsession for toy horses lasted unbroken until real horses became important some years later," she wrote.

JUNE 18, 1946

Princess Elizabeth smiles as she arrives by carriage for Royal Ascot alongside Princess Mary, her aunt. Queen Anne established racing at Ascot in 1711, and the site has since received the patronage of 11 other monarchs. The summer race meeting, which is a five-day showcase of world-class racing, officially became a royal week in 1911, and the tradition of the royal carriage procession was started in 1825. Princess Elizabeth first attended Royal Ascot in 1945 wearing her World War II military uniform. It has been a staple event in her calendar ever since and is often described as one of her favorite times of the year. Now in her 90s, she continues to attend every day of Royal Ascot despite having scaled back some of her other commitments.

NOVEMBER 24, 1947

Newlyweds Princess Elizabeth and Prince Philip play with her pet dog Susan at the start of their honeymoon at Broadlands, in Hampshire. The Princess received Susan, a Welsh corgi, as an 18th birthday present, and many of her other corgis and dorgis are descended from the dog. Lady Pamela Hicks, the daughter of Louis, 1st Earl Mountbatten of Burma, and one of Elizabeth's bridesmaids, wrote in her memoir *Daughter of Empire: Life as a Mountbatten* that the royal bride was "delighted to discover that Susan, her favorite corgi, had been hidden under a rug in her carriage so that she could join them for their honeymoon at Broadlands." Susan died in 1959, and the Queen designed the headstone for the corgi's burial plot on the grounds of Sandringham House. It reads, "For almost 15 years the faithful companion of the Queen."

SEPTEMBER 28, 1952

The Queen stands with one of her corgis at Balmoral Castle, in Scotland. When she moves between residences, her dogs travel with her. They enjoy their own menus of finely chopped meat. The Queen's former dog trainer Roger Mugford once told *Town & Country*, "At feeding times, each dog had an individually designed menu, including an array of homeopathic and herbal remedies. Their food was served by a butler in an eclectic collection of battered silver and porcelain dishes." Mugford continued, "As I watched, the Queen got the corgis to sit in a semicircle around her and then fed them one by one, in order of seniority. The others just sat and patiently waited their turn."

JUNE 1958

ABOVE Princess Margaret, the Queen, and the Queen Mother attend the Epsom Derby, the annual June race meeting at Epsom Downs Racecourse, in Surrey. Elizabeth first attended the event in 1946 with her father. She has missed it only twice during her reign.

JUNE 16, 1961

RIGHT The Queen rides on the racecourse at Royal Ascot before the events begin. In the early years of her reign, the sight of the monarch galloping on horseback in her headscarf and jodhpurs at the start of the races was a familiar one. Other members of her family, including Princess Margaret, would join her.

NOVEMBER 20, 1979

OPPOSITE The Queen and Prince Philip spend time with their children and dogs at Balmoral Castle, in Scotland, in an image released for their 32nd wedding anniversary. Pets have been an essential part of family life for Elizabeth's children and grandchildren. In an interview for the 2012 ITV documentary *Elizabeth: Queen, Wife, and Mother*, Prince William said about his grandmother's dogs, "They're barking all the time.…I don't know how she copes with it. But her private life with her dogs and her riding and her walking, it's very important to her—she has got to switch off. She enjoys it. I would just question the noise!" The corgis have also been known to bite as well as bark. In 1991, the Queen needed three stitches after breaking up a fight between her corgis and her mother's corgis.

1980s

The Royal Mews at Buckingham Palace, which is responsible for all royal road travel arrangements, is home to state coaches and other carriages as well as the horses that pull them. There are approximately 30 horses kept at the Mews, all Windsor Greys or Cleveland Bays. Windsor Greys, so called because they used to be kept at Windsor during the Victorian era, are used to pull royal carriages. Cleveland Bays are used to transport the carriages of high commissioners and ambassadors presenting their credentials to the Queen. The horses also pull carriages carrying the Queen's guests at Royal Ascot. Coaches kept at the Mews include the elaborate Gold State Coach, used for coronations and jubilees, as well as those used at royal weddings and for the state opening of Parliament.

JUNE 1982

The Queen rides on horseback with United States President
Ronald Reagan in Home Park, a private park located on the
grounds of Windsor Castle. President Reagan and his wife, Nancy,
became the first American presidential couple to stay at the castle.
The Queen rode her horse Burmese, and the president borrowed
the stallion Centennial. At the same time, Prince Philip took the
First Lady through Windsor Great Park in a horse-drawn carriage.

MAY 11, 1985

The Queen enjoys the Royal Windsor Horse Show with her daughter, Princess Anne, and grandchildren Peter and Zara Phillips. The annual equestrian competition is held on the grounds of Windsor Castle, and the Queen attends every year. She is usually dressed casually, with a headscarf, and can be spotted watching the horses or wandering around browsing the shopping stalls. Celebration pageants for her Diamond Jubilee and 90th birthday were held at the show.

SEPTEMBER 16, 1998

The Queen's dogs depart an aircraft at Heathrow Airport, in London. As well as moving among her residences, the royal dogs have been such an essential part of the Queen's life that they have even accompanied her on official overseas visits. The Queen's former dog trainer Roger Mugford told *Town & Country* in 2015, "The dogs are bundled in and out of cars and airplanes between these several locations. They are good travelers."

JULY 6, 1999

The Queen greets a guide dog during a garden party in Edinburgh, Scotland. Elizabeth has been patron of the Royal Society of the Prevention of Cruelty to Animals since 1952. Today, she is patron of more than 30 animal charities and organizations worldwide, including Dogs Trust, the British Horse Society, and the Royal Society for the Protection of Birds.

MARCH 27, 2011

Zara Phillips, on her horse Tallyho Sambucca, speaks with her mother, Princess Anne, during the Gatcombe Park horse trials. The Queen passed on her love of horses to Anne, who competed in the 1976 Olympic Games. Anne's daughter, Zara, followed suit, competing in the 2012 Olympic Games in London and winning a silver medal.

JUNE 2, 1993

The Queen watches races at the Epsom Derby alongside guests including the Queen Mother, Prince Charles, and the Earl of Carnarvon. The earl was a close friend of the Queen's and was her racing manager from 1969 until his death in 2001. She called him Porchey, after his courtesy title, Lord Porchester, which he used until he inherited his father's title of Earl of Carnarvon. He was responsible for all the Queen's racing and horse-breeding interests.

APRIL 21, 2005

The Queen rides her Fell pony in Windsor on her 79th birthday. She still rides, well into her 90s, but only ponies. The last horse she used for riding, Sanction, was put down in 2002. In 2020, the Queen's stud groom and manager at Windsor Castle, Terry Pendry, told *Horse & Hound* magazine, "Sanction was the last homebred horse that Her Majesty rode before making the decision to start riding native ponies. A little closer to the ground, so to speak."

OCTOBER 16, 2007

ABOVE Members of the New Zealand rugby league team are greeted by the Queen's dogs as they wait to meet her in the Bow Room at Buckingham Palace. Because information about the Queen's dogs is considered private, Buckingham Palace officials rarely comment on how many she has at any one time. However, in 2007, she was noted to have had five corgis, four dorgis, and five cocker spaniels. In September 2012, Buckingham Palace said that her corgi Monty had died. She was reported to have stopped breeding corgis in 2015 so as not to leave any behind after her death. Willow, then thought to be the Queen's last corgi, died in April 2018. In October 2018, it was reported that Whisper, a corgi she had adopted, had just passed away.

APRIL 2009

OPPOSITE TOP The Queen's dogs are taken for a walk past United States President Barack Obama's car while he has a private audience with the Queen at Buckingham Palace. The corgis have met many world leaders and celebrities. In 2012, they even starred alongside James Bond actor Daniel Craig during the opening ceremony of the London Olympic Games. The Queen featured in a sketch in which Agent 007 arrives at Buckingham Palace to escort her to the Olympic stadium, and her three corgis Monty, Holly, and Willow run along the palace corridors and perform tummy rolls.

LEFT Looking delighted, the Queen watches the horses at Newbury Racecourse alongside her racing manager John Warren (standing), whose full title is the Queen's Bloodstock and Racing Adviser, and trainer Michael Bell. Warren is the son-in-law of the Queen's former racing manager the Earl of Carnarvon; he took over as the Queen's racing manager in 2001, when the earl died. His children are friends with Princes William and Harry, and Warren's granddaughter Zalie Warren was a bridesmaid in Prince Harry and Meghan Markle's wedding in 2018.

JUNE 20, 2013

The Queen and jockey Ryan Moore celebrate winning the Gold Cup at Royal Ascot with her horse Estimate. This was a historic moment—the first time the Gold Cup race had been won by a reigning monarch. The Queen inherited breeding and racing stock from her father in 1952 and continues to raise racehorses. Today, the horses are foaled at the Royal Stud on the Sandringham Estate, in Norfolk, England, and then raised and trained elsewhere. The Queen takes a keen interest in their development. Her registered racing colors, worn by the jockeys riding her horses, are purple with gold braiding, red sleeves, and a black cap with gold fringe.

MARCH 17, 2015

The Queen and Prince Philip attend the opening of the new Mary Tealby Kennels at Battersea Dogs and Cats Home. During this visit, she was asked whether she was tempted to take home a corgi; she replied, "Not at the moment, no." The Queen was patron of the charity from 1956 until 2016, when she announced that she would be handing over some of her patronages due to her advancing years. The Duchess of Cornwall became the organization's new patron in 2017. When the Queen's patronage ended, the charity's chief executive said, "Thank you from all our dogs and cats, Ma'am. You've helped ensure our vital work and our contribution to society is fully recognized on the world stage."

OCTOBER 29, 2015

The Queen's dog sits at her feet as she speaks with Prime Minister John Key, of New Zealand, during a Windsor Castle audience. Her dogs, as well as being present for official meetings, have even sometimes been involved with her duties. In a 2016 BBC Radio 4 interview, war surgeon David Nott described meeting the Queen at a luncheon after his return from Syria in 2014. When she saw he was struggling to speak about his experiences there, she suggested that he join her in feeding her dogs instead. He said, "All of a sudden, the courtiers brought the corgis, and the corgis went underneath the table.…And so for 20 minutes, the Queen and I, during this lunch, fed the dogs. She did it because she knew that I was so seriously traumatized. You know, the humanity of what she was doing was unbelievable."

Members of the royal family arrive in the parade ring during the carriage procession at Royal Ascot. Each day of the summer race meeting begins with the carriage procession at 2 p.m., a tradition started by King George IV in 1825. Racegoers line the route and gather in the parade ring to catch a glimpse of the Queen and her guests in Ascot Landau carriages pulled by Windsor Grey and Cleveland Bay horses.

CHAPTER NINE

A Palace to Call Home

"WELL, YOU DO RATHER HOPE THE SUN SHINES, AS WHEN YOU INVITE 8,000 PEOPLE TO HAVE TEA ON YOUR LAWN, IT CAN BE A BIT OF A WORRY."

— The Queen, to a guest at a Buckingham Palace garden party, May 2019

SEPTEMBER 1952

The Queen helps two-year-old Princess Anne climb through a window at Balmoral Castle, in Scotland, as three-year-old Prince Charles stands below.

From the iconic Buckingham Palace, in the center of London, to the secluded Balmoral Castle, set on 50,000 acres of Scottish countryside, the Queen's homes make a spectacular backdrop for both duty and leisure. The royal residences across the United Kingdom are steeped in history, and each has a unique charter and purpose.

The British monarch's official residence is 775-room Buckingham Palace. The Queen spends most of her working week here, and it's where many of her staff members have their offices. The palace's magnificent state rooms, among them the ballroom and Throne Room, are used for official entertaining and ceremonial events. The Queen has her own private apartments within the palace, and she and Prince Philip are the only members of the royal family to live there. Other senior royals have their own official residences. When in London, Prince Charles and the Duchess of Cornwall live and work in Clarence House, and the Duke and Duchess of Cambridge have their home and staff at Kensington Palace.

More than 50,000 people visit Buckingham Palace every year as guests for banquets, lunches, receptions, dinners, garden parties, and investitures. When the Queen travels to Scotland every summer, Buckingham Palace's state rooms are open to the paying public alongside a specially curated exhibition. On special occasions, such as jubilees, the palace has also been home to parties and picnics with thousands of people invited onto the grounds.

On weekends, and for about one month surrounding Easter, the Queen is most often found at Windsor Castle, which is just over 20 miles from London. It is the oldest and largest occupied castle in the world, dating back to the reign of William the Conqueror, in the 11th century.

The Queen spends one week every year at her official Scottish residence, the Palace of Holyroodhouse, in Edinburgh. When she visits Northern Ireland, she resides in Hillsborough Castle and Gardens, located just outside Belfast. She does not have an official residence in Wales.

In addition to her official residences, the Queen also has two private properties where she spends time out of the spotlight: Balmoral Castle, in the Scottish Highlands, and Sandringham House, in Norfolk, England. Elizabeth stays at Sandringham each Christmas and remains there until after February 6, the anniversary of her father's death and of her accession.

The royal family spends August and September at Balmoral Castle. Away from the spotlight, they enjoy country pursuits— riding, shooting, bracing walks, and picnics. In ITV documentary *Our Queen at Ninety*, Elizabeth's granddaughter Princess Eugenie described the Scottish retreat: "It's a lovely base for Granny and Grandpa, for us to come and see them up there, where you just have room to breathe and run. It's the most beautiful place on Earth. I think Granny is the most happy there."

BUCKINGHAM PALACE

JUNE 27, 2018

The Band of the Coldstream Guards during the Changing of the Guard ceremony at Buckingham Palace. Buckingham Palace was first built as a townhouse for the Duke of Buckingham and Normanby in 1703 and then purchased by King George III in 1761 as a family home for his wife, Queen Charlotte, and their children. It was remodeled extensively by his son King George IV, who placed architect John Nash in charge of the work. However, it wasn't until Queen Victoria came to the throne, in 1837, that the palace became the official London residence of the British monarch. Upon Prince Albert's suggestion, architect Edward Blore created the now iconic central balcony at the front of the palace. Today, the palace's 775 rooms include 19 state rooms, 52 royal and guest bedrooms, 188 staff bedrooms, 92 offices, and 78 bathrooms. The palace is home to more than 800 members of staff, including housekeepers, catering staff, footmen, gardeners, and the teams who handle official correspondence. It contains five main departments with offices: the Private Secretary's Office, which supports the Queen in her official duties; the Privy Purse and Treasurer's Office, which includes finance and information technology; the Master of the Household, which handles hospitality and housekeeping; the Lord Chamberlain's Office, which organizes ceremonial activities; and the Royal Collection Trust, which oversees the Royal Collection, the largest private art collection in the world, as well as its public openings and exhibitions. Buckingham Palace also has a swimming pool, which can be used by members of the royal family and staff. The state rooms are open to visitors for 10 weeks each summer. When the Queen is in residence, the Royal Standard flag flies above the palace; when she is away, the Union Jack is flown instead. In 2016, it was announced that Buckingham Palace would undergo a major 10-year reservicing program to carry out urgent repairs. The decision sparked some criticism when £369 million of public money was pledged to the project. The work began in April 2017.

JUNE 27, 1927

An infant Princess Elizabeth is surrounded by her parents, then the Duke and Duchess of York, and her grandparents King George V and Queen Mary on the balcony of Buckingham Palace. Balcony appearances have been a tradition in the royal family since 1851, when Queen Victoria stepped onto it during celebrations for the opening of the Great Exhibition, the first international fair of culture and industry. When her eldest daughter, Princess Victoria, was married in 1858, the newlyweds used the balcony to acknowledge the crowds below, and it has been an integral part of prominent royal weddings ever since.

JULY 19, 1946

Princess Elizabeth at her desk in her office at Buckingham Palace. The Queen's private offices and apartments at the palace have rarely been photographed. Despite round-the-clock protection by London's Metropolitan Police Service, there have been several security breaches. The most notable one was at about 7 a.m. on July 9, 1982, when Michael Fagan climbed over the palace fence and up a drainpipe and made his way to the Queen's private apartments, where he found her in bed alone. Initial reports said that Fagan spent 10 minutes talking to her; however, he said in a 2012 newspaper interview in the *Independent on Sunday* that the Queen ran straight past him. He was arrested after the Queen raised the alarm and a footman stayed with him until police arrived. Fagan had broken into the palace a month earlier and spent the night there undetected; by his own account, he sat on a throne, wandered around, and drank wine. Trespassing was then a civil wrong, not a criminal offense, and Fagan was not charged. He was later acquitted of stealing the wine. After Fagan admitted to stealing a car (a crime unrelated to his palace break-in), he was sent to a high-security mental health hospital for three months in October 1982. Home Secretary William Whitelaw offered his resignation over Fagan's Buckingham Palace security breach, but it was refused.

JULY 10, 1947

Princess Elizabeth and Philip Mountbatten attend a garden party at Buckingham Palace shortly after their engagement was announced. The tradition of garden parties dates back to the 1860s during the reign of Queen Victoria. Today, there are usually four garden parties held annually, three at Buckingham Palace and one at the Palace of Holyroodhouse in Edinburgh, Scotland. Almost 8,000 guests attend each party, comprising people from all walks of life who have made a positive impact on their communities.

JULY 21, 1998

The Queen and Prince Philip prepare to greet guests at a Buckingham Palace garden party. According to the palace, at each party, an estimated 27,000 cups of tea are served along with 20,000 sandwiches and 20,000 slices of cake. The royal family arrives to the sound of the national anthem and then mingles with their guests.

JUNE 14, 2009

The Queen and Prince Philip along with Deputy Gardens Manager Claire Midgley look over the vegetable garden on the grounds of Buckingham Palace. The palace garden covers 16 hectares and is home to 30 species of birds, more than 300 types of wildflowers, and more than 150 mature trees. It also has a 3-acre lake and a tennis court. Every Monday morning when the Queen is in residence, the gardens manager sends her a bouquet of freshly gathered flowers. In the 2018 ITV documentary *The Queen's Green Planet*, Elizabeth toured the Buckingham Palace garden with Sir David Attenborough and hinted at her frustration with the aircraft flying above. When one was heard overhead, she remarked, "Why do they always go round and round when you want to talk?" The Queen also showed Attenborough the oak trees that were planted upon the birth of each of her four children.

JUNE 4, 2012

A couple enjoys a picnic on the grounds of Buckingham Palace during the Diamond Jubilee celebrations. The palace doors were opened to 12,000 members of the public, who were all given picnic baskets created specially for the occasion in consultation with royal chef Mark Flanagan.

JULY 12, 2012

ABOVE Aerial view of Buckingham Palace and the Mall.

JUNE 24, 2015

RIGHT Tourists watch Changing of the Guard on the forecourt of Buckingham Palace. This striking display of pageantry has been a huge tourist attraction. Also known as Guard Mounting, it is a highly choreographed ceremony in which the Queen's guard hands over the responsibility of protecting the palace to the new guard. The Queen's guard is usually provided by one of the five regiments of foot guards from the Household Division, which has protected the sovereign and royal palaces since 1660.

Guests attend a state banquet in the Buckingham Palace ballroom for the King and Queen of Spain. The banquet is the centerpiece of a state visit, when the United Kingdom rolls out the red carpet for visiting heads of state. Planning for the banquet can start as far as a year in advance, and the preparations for the table begin five days ahead. The Master of the Household's department is responsible for running the event, but every element of the banquet, from the seating plan to the menu, is personally overseen and approved by the Queen. The table is set with the Grand Service, a silver-gilt dining service commissioned in the 19th century by King George IV before he became king. It comprises more than 4,000 pieces, from elaborate dessert stands to trays and egg cups.

WINDSOR CASTLE

JUNE 10, 2020

A view of Windsor Castle from the Long Walk, a 2.5-mile stretch that connects the castle to Windsor Great Park. Windsor Castle was first built by William the Conqueror in the 11th century and has been home to 39 monarchs. Originally constructed as a fortress to guard the western approach to London, it was remodeled by royals throughout the centuries to become the lavish residence it is today. The castle grounds occupy 13 acres and the castle has about 1,000 rooms, including grand state apartments used for investitures and other official occasions. It sits next to Home Park, which houses private gardens and other royal residences including Frogmore House and Frogmore Cottage. The castle property contains St. George's Chapel, where many royal weddings have been held, including Prince Harry and Meghan Markle's in 2018. The chapel is also the burial place of several members of the royal family, including 10 former British monarchs. The first to be buried there was King Edward IV in 1483, and it is also the resting place of King Henry VIII and his third wife, Jane Seymour. The Queen's father, mother, and sister are also interred there, in the King George VI Memorial Chapel.

MAY 18, 1961

The Queen and young Prince Charles ride at Windsor Castle, which serves as the Queen's weekend retreat. She has often been photographed riding her horses in the adjacent Home Park and in nearby Windsor Great Park. When Prince William was at Eton College, he visited his grandmother at the castle on weekends for tea.

APRIL 21, 1968

The Queen, Prince Philip, and their four children take a walk on the grounds of Frogmore House, in Windsor. A royal residence since 1792, Frogmore House was originally used by Queen Charlotte, the wife of King George III, as a country retreat. Queen Victoria's mother lived there until she died in 1861, and King George VI and the Queen Mother spent part of their honeymoon there. Its gardens include the Royal Burial Ground and the Royal Mausoleum, where Queen Victoria and Prince Albert are laid to rest. Nearby is the burial place of King Edward VIII and Wallis Simpson. Frogmore Cottage, a former staff quarters that was renovated to become the British home of the Duke and Duchess of Sussex, is also located here.

APRIL 12, 1977

The Queen looks over her diary of engagements in her Windsor Castle sitting room. While her main office is in Buckingham Palace, the Queen works from all her residences, with the daily red boxes of government papers sent to her wherever she is. All her homes are decorated with photographs of her family.

NOVEMBER 20, 1992

Firefighters battle the flames lapping Windsor Castle, a blaze that lasted for 15 hours. It started in Queen Victoria's Private Chapel, where a spotlight ignited a curtain. Staff members were able to remove valuable works of art from the fire's path, but it went on to ravage 115 rooms, including nine state apartments. It was finally extinguished in the early hours of November 21 and left a huge restoration task in its aftermath. Prince Philip chaired the restoration committee, and the project took five years to complete. The year of the fire was a particularly challenging one for the Queen: Three of her four children divorced or separated, and a book detailing Princess Diana's unhappiness in the royal family was published. In a November speech, the Queen said, "Nineteen ninety-two is not a year on which I shall look back with undiluted pleasure. In the words of one of my more sympathetic correspondents, it has turned out to be an 'annus horribilis.'"

BALMORAL CASTLE

DECEMBER 2019

Snow blankets Balmoral Castle. Set on a 50,000-acre estate in Royal Deeside, Aberdeenshire, the castle has been used by the royal family as their Scottish retreat since Queen Victoria and Prince Albert purchased it in 1852. They decided to build a new castle on the site, which was completed in 1856. Prince Albert took a great interest in landscaping and improving the area, and when he died in 1861, Victoria continued the work. She spent much time at the property, which has been enjoyed by successive monarchs and their families. Prince Philip has taken an active role in managing and improving the estate, where he and Elizabeth still spend their summers and are joined by other family members. It is a working estate, with deer stalking, grouse shooting, forestry, and farming. It is also home to Highland cattle and ponies. Prince Charles has a residence on the estate, Birkhall, which he inherited from the Queen Mother. Balmoral Castle is open to the public from April until July every year.

1912

King George V shoots at Balmoral Castle, beside the River Dee. Today, the royal family's enjoyment of shooting is a more controversial topic than it was 100 years ago. Despite criticism from animal rights groups, however, they continue to participate in the sport and hold shooting parties at Balmoral and Sandringham.

1929

Princess Elizabeth watches musicians perform during a visit to Balmoral Castle. The Queen still enjoys listening to bagpipes and has a piper play outside her bedroom window for 15 minutes at 9 o'clock every morning at every residence except Sandringham. The piper to the sovereign also plays on state occasions. The tradition goes back to the time of Queen Victoria, who decided she wanted one after she visited the Marquis of Breadalbane at Taymouth Castle and heard the pipers play.

The Queen (left) dancing with a friend on the Balmoral Estate. Royal family members are often at their most informal and relaxed during their visits to the Scottish Highlands, where they enjoy eating outdoors. The Queen is understood to enjoy a gin and Dubonnet cocktail before lunch.

SEPTEMBER 1971

The Queen dances at the Ghillies Ball at Balmoral Castle. Elizabeth hosts the annual get-together in the castle's ballroom. It's attended by the royal family, estate staff, and members of the community. The Queen enjoys Scottish country dancing, and the ball has often opened with her joining an eightsome reel.

SANDRINGHAM HOUSE

OCTOBER 3, 2006

Sandringham House and grounds, a country home for British royals since 1862. Set within the 8,000-hectare Sandringham Estate, in Norfolk, Sandringham House was acquired by King Edward VII when he was the Prince of Wales. The Queen's grandfather King George V referred to it as "dear old Sandringham, the place I love better than anywhere else in the world." And her father, King George VI, said, "I have always been so happy here, and I love the place." It was the location for the first-ever royal Christmas message, which was broadcast live on the radio in 1932. It was also where King George VI died in his sleep on February 6, 1952. In the earlier years of her reign, the Queen spent many Christmases at Windsor Castle, but since 1988, she has celebrated the holiday at Sandringham.

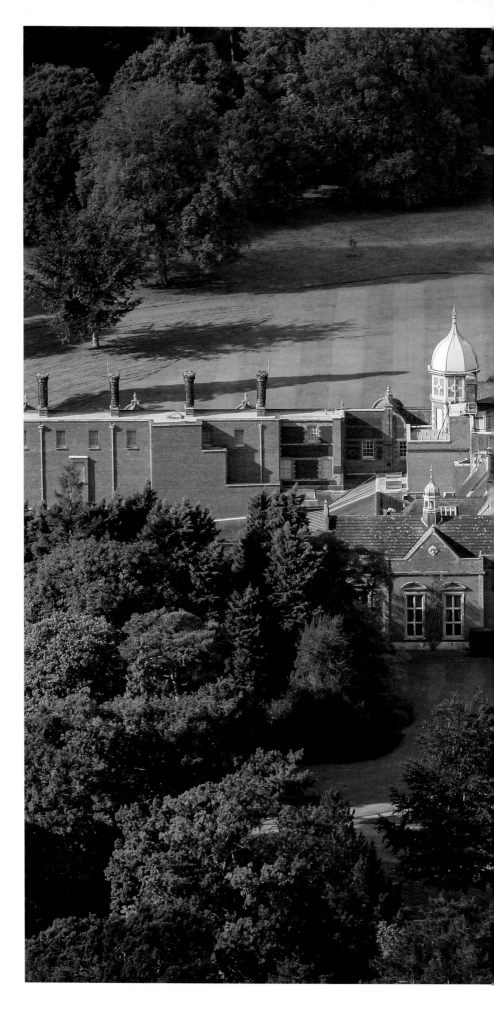

DECEMBER 25, 2012

The Queen receives flowers from children as she leaves St. Mary Magdalene Church, in Norfolk, following the Christmas Day service. Members of the royal family walk from Sandringham House to church for the 11 a.m. service on Christmas Day before returning for lunch. The family follows the German tradition of opening presents on Christmas Eve, and there is a shooting party held on Boxing Day, the day after Christmas. The Queen and Prince Philip send about 750 Christmas cards each year. The Queen personally hands out presents to some staff members and follows a tradition started by her grandfather of giving Christmas puddings to palace workers.

DECEMBER 21, 2017

OPPOSITE The Queen and Prince Philip arrive at King's Lynn station by train from London for her Christmas holiday. Each year, she takes the train from London to Norfolk, where she is driven to Sandringham. For many, the sight of the Queen in her headscarf standing on the platform signals the beginning of the festive season.

THE PALACE OF
HOLYROODHOUSE

JULY 12, 2010

The Ceremony of the Keys at the Palace of
Holyroodhouse, an event that welcomes the Queen
to Edinburgh, Scotland, at the beginning of each
of her stays. Edinburgh's lord provost symbolically
offers the Queen the keys to the city. She responds,
"I return these keys, being perfectly convinced that
they cannot be placed in better hands than those
of the lord provost and councillors of my good city
of Edinburgh."

JULY 1, 2014

The Queen attends a garden party at the Palace of
Holyroodhouse, her official residence in Scotland.
It is situated at the end of Edinburgh's Royal Mile
against the spectacular backdrop of extinct volcano
Arthur's Seat. The site was founded as a monastery,
and later, the abbey housed royal chambers used by
the sovereign. At around the start of the 16th century,
King James IV of Scotland converted these into a
palace. One of its most famous residents was Mary,
Queen of Scots, who lived there from 1561 to 1567,
when she was imprisoned, was forced to abdicate,
and eventually fled from Scotland. According
to the royal household, the Queen's grandfather
King George V hosted the first garden party at
Holyroodhouse in 1911, a tradition that carries on
today. Every summer, the Queen spends one week
at the palace, receiving audiences and carrying out
official visits in Scotland.

HILLSBOROUGH CASTLE AND GARDENS

DECEMBER 8, 2005

ABOVE The Queen and Prince Philip greet President of Ireland Mary McAleese and her husband, Martin, at Hillsborough Castle, in County Down, Northern Ireland. Hillsborough is a royal residence and also the official home of the secretary of state for Northern Ireland. The Georgian country house, built in the 18th century, was sold to the British government in 1925. It has 100 acres of gardens and is open to the public most of the year.

AUGUST 2016

RIGHT Hillsborough Castle in the summer.

Commemoration and Celebration

"THE WARTIME GENERATION KNEW THAT THE BEST WAY TO HONOR THOSE WHO DID NOT COME BACK FROM THE WAR WAS TO ENSURE THAT IT DIDN'T HAPPEN AGAIN."

— The Queen, during her address to mark the 75th anniversary of Victory in Europe Day, May 8, 2020

JUNE 3, 2012

A flotilla of boats, which includes a barge carrying the Queen and members of her family, marks the Queen's Diamond Jubilee in a river pageant down the River Thames, London, as crowds gather to watch. The event was one among many events celebrating the Queen's 60 years on the throne, which also included a service of thanksgiving, a picnic in the garden of Buckingham Palace, and a concert in front of the palace.

The Queen has been at the heart of British national life in times of celebration and sorrow. As well as holding the official position of head of state, with its constitutional duties and other formally prescribed routines, she is also described as being the head of nation. This is a less defined or formal role, but it expresses the fact that she represents national unity, continuity, and stability. For many Britons who have never known another monarch, the Queen's presence is an integral part of national life.

Every year, the Queen leads the nation in honoring the war dead at the Cenotaph, in London, as well as at other important occasions of national remembrance. Increasingly, younger royal family members represent the Queen at overseas events, such as when Prince Charles and the Duchess of Cornwall visited Normandy, France, in June 2019 for the 75th anniversary of the D-Day landings.

"Inevitably, a long life can pass by many milestones. My own is no exception," the Queen said in a rare personal speech when she became the longest-reigning British monarch in 2015, overtaking the previous record held by Queen Victoria of 63 years, seven months, and two days.

Elizabeth's significant milestones have been celebrated as grand occasions. An international lighting ceremony marked her Diamond Jubilee in June 2012. The first beacon was lit in Marlborough, New Zealand, starting a chain that progressed around the world. More than 4,200 beacons were lit across the Commonwealth nations, ending with the Queen's lighting the National Beacon on the Mall, in London. During an address to Parliament for her Diamond Jubilee, the Queen reaffirmed her lifelong commitment to duty, saying, "We are reminded here of our past, of the continuity of our national story and the virtues of resilience, ingenuity, and tolerance which created it. I have been privileged to witness some of that history and, with the support of my family, rededicate myself to the service of our great country and its people now and in the years to come."

The monarchy's ongoing appeal is evident in the global interest in the lives and work of the younger royals. However, for many, it is the Queen who remains its star. Polls consistently find her to be the most popular royal, with a high approval rating among the British public. She is now in her 90s and still carrying out her duties, and it is this steadfast dedication that has earned her a place in so many people's hearts.

MAY 8, 1945

Princess Elizabeth joins her parents, King George VI and Queen Elizabeth, her sister Princess Margaret, and Prime Minister Winston Churchill on the balcony of Buckingham Palace on Victory in Europe Day. After the picture was taken, Princesses Elizabeth and Margaret went out incognito to celebrate with the crowds. In a BBC radio program in 1985, the Queen described it as "one of the most memorable nights of my life." She admitted she was terrified of being recognized and said, "We cheered the King and Queen on the balcony and then walked miles through the street. I remember lines of unknown people linking arms and walking down Whitehall, all of us just swept along on a tide of happiness and relief."

NOVEMBER 11, 1945

Princess Elizabeth lays a wreath for the first time at the Cenotaph, in London, on Remembrance Sunday. She has done so almost every year since, except for four occasions when she was overseas and twice when she was pregnant. Since 2017, in a concession to her advancing years, Prince Charles has laid a wreath on her behalf while the Queen watches from a nearby balcony.

JUNE 13, 1964

The Queen holds her youngest child, Prince Edward, at three months old, on the balcony of Buckingham Palace during her official birthday parade, Trooping the Colour. The Queen's actual birthday is April 21, but the occasion is marked officially on the second Saturday in June. The tradition of the sovereign having two birthdays began with King George II in 1748. His birthday was in November, but he moved the celebrations to coincide with an annual military parade in the summer.

JUNE 7, 1977

The Queen rides in the Gold State Coach past crowds lining the streets in central London during her Silver Jubilee celebrations. Commemorative events took place up and down the country to mark her 25 years on the throne, with the main celebrations held in June in London. She attended a service of thanksgiving at St. Paul's Cathedral before giving a speech during a lunch at the Guildhall. She said, "When I was 21, I pledged my life to the service of our people, and I asked for God's help to make good that vow. Although that vow was made in my salad days when I was green in judgment, I do not regret nor retract one word of it."

APRIL 25, 1988

The Queen meets war veterans in Hobart, Tasmania, Australia, on Anzac Day, the anniversary of the landings of the Australian and New Zealand Army Corps at Gallipoli, Turkey, on April 25, 1915, during World War I. The day pays tribute to Anzacs who served and died in all wars, conflicts, and peacekeeping operations. Members of the royal family recognize the day in the United Kingdom and have also joined commemorations in Australia and New Zealand when on visits there.

NOVEMBER 19, 1997

The Queen wears a golden dress for her golden wedding anniversary celebrations. She is accompanied by Prince Philip and Prince Edward. The milestone was marked with two days of events in London. On the eve of the anniversary, the Queen and Philip attended a lunch at the Guildhall and then a gala concert at Royal Festival Hall. On the anniversary itself, November 20, 1997, the couple attended a service of thanksgiving at Westminster Abbey. During lunch at the Guildhall, the Queen made one of her most famous speeches, in which she described Philip as her "strength and stay."

AUGUST 4, 2000

Princess Margaret, the Queen Mother, and the Queen on the balcony of Buckingham Palace on the Queen Mother's 100th birthday. She became the first member of the royal family ever to reach that milestone, and celebrations were held throughout the day. The Queen Mother received a message from her daughter Elizabeth, a personalized version of the telegram the Queen sends to all centenarians. It was signed "Lilibet," Elizabeth's childhood nickname. More than 40,000 well-wishers gathered on the Mall to watch the Queen Mother appear on the Buckingham Palace balcony to the sound of the Coldstream Guards playing "Happy Birthday."

JUNE 4, 2002

The Queen waves to the crowds gathered on the Mall, in London, during the Golden Jubilee celebrations. The year began as a difficult one for the Queen: Her mother and sister died within a few weeks of each other in February and March. However, her jubilee was cause for great celebration, with four days of events taking place over a weekend in June as well as visits throughout the year to 70 cities in the United Kingdom and several overseas destinations. The highlights included a classical music concert on the grounds of Buckingham Palace, jubilee church services held around the United Kingdom and Commonwealth, street parties throughout the United Kingdom, and a procession to a thanksgiving service at St. Paul's Cathedral. A rock concert, "Party at the Palace," took place on the gardens of Buckingham Palace and included performances by Paul McCartney, Shirley Bassey, Tom Jones, and Queen. In a June speech, the Queen said, "It has been a pretty remarkable 50 years by any standards. There have been ups and downs, but anyone who can remember what things were like after those six long years of war appreciates what immense changes have been achieved since then."

APRIL 9, 2005

The royal family descends the steps of St. George's Chapel after the Service of Prayer and Dedication to mark the marriage of Prince Charles and Camilla Parker Bowles, in Windsor. The couple had just received the blessing from the Archbishop of Canterbury following their civil wedding at the Windsor Guildhall. Crowds of 20,000 took to the streets to cheer them, even though polling at the time revealed a split in public opinion over whether they should marry. Polls also found that most respondents did not think Camilla should have the title of queen once Prince Charles becomes king. At the time of their marriage, the palace announced that when Prince Charles takes the throne, Camilla would instead be known as princess consort. However, legally, she would become queen consort, and many believe that Prince Charles would want her to use that title. Recent polls show that Camilla's popularity with the public has grown, although reactions to her using the title of queen remain mixed.

JUNE 14, 2008

Members of the royal family stand on the balcony of Buckingham Palace during the Queen's annual official birthday parade, Trooping the Colour. The Band of the Household Cavalry is playing below and the Royal Standard flag can be seen flying from the palace, indicating that the Queen is in residence.

JULY 6, 2010

The Queen pays her respects after laying a wreath in remembrance of the victims of the September 11 attacks in New York. The Queen visited the site of the World Trade Center and met families of the victims. She also opened the British Garden in New York's Hanover Square to memorialize the 67 British citizens who lost their lives on 9/11. During her visit, the Queen addressed the United Nations General Assembly, where she closed her speech by saying, "In tomorrow's world, we must all work together as hard as ever if we are truly to be united nations."

APRIL 29, 2011

Prince William and Kate Middleton wave to the crowds on their way to Buckingham Palace following their wedding service at Westminster Abbey. The day was a public holiday in the United Kingdom, and an estimated one million people lined the route of the carriage procession. More than 5,000 street parties were held across the country, and the marriage was celebrated globally, with an estimated two billion people worldwide watching the event on television. A few months later, the Queen's granddaughter Zara Phillips married Mike Tindall in Edinburgh, Scotland. In her Christmas message that year, the Queen said, "The importance of family has, of course, come home to Prince Philip and me personally this year with the marriages of two of our grandchildren, each in their own way a celebration of the God-given love that binds a family together."

JUNE 5, 2012

Crowds gather outside Buckingham Palace as the Royal Air Force performs a flyover on the Queen's Diamond Jubilee. The celebrations took place over an extended public holiday weekend in June. Events included a picnic for 12,000 people on the grounds of Buckingham Palace followed by a concert out front. To mark the occasion, the Queen was transported down the River Thames aboard a specially decorated royal barge in a flotilla of 1,000 boats. The Queen turned 86 in her Diamond Jubilee year and did not travel overseas as she had done in previous jubilee years. Instead, younger members of her family visited the Commonwealth realms while Elizabeth toured the United Kingdom. In an address to both houses of Parliament in March 2012, the Queen referenced the fact that Queen Victoria was the only other British monarch to have marked 60 years on the throne, saying, "So, in an era when the regular, worthy rhythm of life is less eye-catching than doing something extraordinary, I am reassured that I am merely the second sovereign to celebrate a Diamond Jubilee."

JUNE 6, 2014

ABOVE The Queen bows her head after laying a wreath at Bayeux War Cemetery, in Normandy, France, during commemorations for the 70th anniversary of the D-Day landings. It was a rare foreign trip for the Queen since she scaled back her travel in 2013. She joined veterans of the Normandy invasion for this poignant service, which marked the Allied landing in France during World War II.

OCTOBER 16, 2014

LEFT The Queen stands among a sea of ceramic poppies at the Tower of London. Art installation Blood Swept Lands and Seas of Red marked the centenary of the outbreak of World War I. By November 11, 2014, 888,246 poppies had been planted in the tower's moat—one for each British or Colonial death during the conflict.

ABOVE AND OPPOSITE The Queen and Prince Philip travel
down the Mall during a lunch for 10,000 people connected to her
patronages to celebrate her 90th birthday year. The Queen remains
patron of more than 600 charities and organizations, although
when she turned 90, she began to hand over some of these to
younger members of the family. She usually spends her actual
birthday privately, but on the day she turned 90, on April 21, 2016,
the Queen unveiled a plaque in Windsor and greeted crowds.
Celebrations were held throughout the year. The Queen said in
a speech that June, "I much appreciate the kindness of all your
birthday wishes and have been delighted and moved by the many
cards and messages I have received. How I will feel if people are still
singing 'Happy Birthday' to me in December remains to be seen!"

The Queen on the balcony of the United Kingdom's Foreign and Commonwealth Office during the annual Remembrance Sunday service at the Cenotaph, in central London. On Remembrance Sunday, members of the royal family join political leaders, religious leaders and dignitaries, members of the British Armed Forces, and military veterans at the Cenotaph memorial. When Big Ben, the bell of the famous Westminster clock, tolls 11 a.m., a single gun is fired on Horse Guards Parade and two minutes of silence are held for the fallen.

MAY 19, 2018

Prince Harry and Meghan Markle share a kiss as they leave St. George's Chapel, in Windsor, following their wedding. The marriage was celebrated throughout the United Kingdom and the world as Meghan made history as the first biracial person to marry into the House of Windsor. The service was watched by an estimated 1.9 billion people worldwide, and an estimated 150,000 people flocked to Windsor to line the route of the carriage procession. The couple waved to crowds as they traveled through the town, down the Long Walk, and back to Windsor Castle for their wedding reception. A private evening reception was held in Frogmore House next to the castle.

NOVEMBER 10, 2018

Members of the royal family attend the annual Festival of Remembrance at the Royal Albert Hall. The annual performance commemorates all those who have lost their lives in conflicts and ends with thousands of poppies being dropped from the roof of the grand concert hall. In 2018, the event was particularly meaningful because it was the 100th anniversary of the armistice that ended World War I in 1918.

JUNE 5, 2019

The Queen attends the commemorations for the 75th anniversary of D-Day alongside Prince Charles, United States President Donald Trump, and First Lady Melania Trump. Leaders from 16 nations participated in the service in Portsmouth, England, where they were joined by 300 surviving veterans of the Normandy landings. In her speech, the Queen praised the "heroism, courage, and sacrifice" of those who lost their lives and added, "It is with humility and pleasure, on behalf of the entire country—indeed, the whole free world—that I say to you all, thank you."

INDEX

A

Albert (prince), 127, 159, 163, 192, 202, 204
Alcázar palace, 87
Aldrin, Buzz, 104
Alexandra (queen), 157, 159
Alice (princess), 34, 153
Amies, Hardy, 121, 129
Andrew (prince)
    birth of, 42
    family life of, 44–45, 59, 61, 202
    honeymoon of, 83
    military service of, 63
    residence of, 52
    stepping down from royal duties, 63
Anne (princess)
    birth of, 42
    childhood of, 42, 44–46, 48–49, 56–59, 79–80, 99, 188–189, 202
    christening of, 55
    as equestrian, 62, 171, 180
    at equestrian events, 179–180
    marriage of, 83, 153
    royal duties of, 69, 104
Anzac Day, 222
Armstrong-Jones, Antony, 61, 83
Armstrong, Neil, 104
Attenborough, David, 196
Australia, 79, 84, 86, 89, 145, 222
Australian and New Zealand Army Corps (ANZAC), 222
Auxiliary Territorial Service, 8–9, 11

B

Badminton Horse Trials, 61
Bahamas, 82–83
Balmoral Castle
    as family retreat, 42, 46, 50, 56–57, 176–177, 191
    history of, 204–205
    hunting at, 206
    music and dancing at, 206–207
Balmoral tartan, 127
Bandeau Tiara, 161
Bangladesh, 82
Barbados, 86
Baring Ruby Necklace, 159
Barlow, Amy, 28
Bassey, Shirley, 112
Battersea Dogs and Cats Home, 184
Bayeux War Cemetery, 229
Beatles, 102–103
Beaton, Cecil, 2, 5
Beatrice (princess), 153
Beefeaters, 146
Bell, Michael, 183
Benedict XVI (pope), 98
Bergen-Belsen concentration camp, 92
Bhumibol (king), 104
Birkhall, 39, 204
Bodmer, Gerald, 126
Botswana, 85
Boucheron Honeycomb Tiara, 154
Brabourne (lord), 35
Brandreth, Gyles, 33, 41
Brazil, 167
Brexit, 141
British Garden memorial (New York City), 227
Buckingham Palace
    about, 190, 192
    balcony photos (formal), 1, 5, 9, 73, 135, 194, 218, 226
    balcony photos (informal), 66, 147, 194, 219, 223
    Diamond Jubilee celebration at, 228
    exterior of, 47, 192–193, 195–198, 226, 228
    interior of, 29, 62, 93, 102–104, 107, 113–114, 116, 136–137, 182, 194, 199, 203
    as the Queen's childhood home, 13
    as the Queen's residence, 39, 61
    security breaches, 194
    stables, 177
    World War II bombing of, 14
Burma (now Myanmar), 159
Burmese (horse), 168–169, 171, 178
Burmese Ruby Tiara, 159, 166
Bush, George H. W., 132
Bush, George W., 89
Bush, Laura, 89

C

Cambridge, Duchess of.
    See also Middleton, Catherine "Kate"
    jewelry worn by, 153–155, 158, 164, 166
    on the Queen, 51, 69–70
    residence of, 68, 190
    royal duties of, 111
    style of, 129, 137, 140
    wedding of, 68, 153
Cambridge, Duke of.
    See William (prince)
Cameron, David, 99
Canada
    brooch symbolizing, 145
    gifts from, 168–169
    state visits to, 16, 24, 81, 154, 164
    walkabouts and, 21
Cape Town speech (1947), 9, 15, 78
Carnarvon, Earl of ("Porchey"), 181, 183
Cartier Halo Tiara (Scroll Tiara), 160
Cenotaph memorial, 16, 219, 232
Ceremony of the Keys, 212
Changing of the Guard, 92–193, 198
Chaplin, Charlie, 98
Charles (prince)
    birth of, 39, 162
    childhood of, 42, 44–45, 48–49, 55–59, 79–80, 99, 127, 188–189, 202
    as equestrian, 171, 202
    at equestrian events, 181
    first marriage of, 62, 64–65, 83
    investiture ceremony for, 60
    mentor of, 43
    at Prince Harry's wedding, 71
    residences of, 190, 204
    royal duties of, 91, 93, 137, 216, 219, 233
    second marriage of, 67, 225
Charles II (king), 73, 144, 146
Charlotte (princess), 51, 68, 70
Charlotte (queen), 202
Charteris (lord), 33
China, 77, 86
Christmas broadcast, 28–29, 81, 95, 106, 165, 208, 227
Christmas traditions, 50, 70, 191, 210–211
Churchill, Winston, 99, 158, 218
Clarence House, 39, 61, 64, 163, 190
Cleveland Bays, 177, 186–187

Cocos (Keeling) Islands, 79
Collins, Michael, 104
Commonwealth of Nations,
    10–11, 16, 41, 75, 77,
    82–83, 86–87, 93, 217.
    *See also specific
    nations*
Como, Perry, 107
Constantine I (king), 34
corgis. See dogs
Cornwall, Duchess of. *See also
    Parker Bowles, Camilla*
  jewelry worn by, 154–155, 164
  marriage of, 67
  residence of, 190
  royal duties of, 184, 216
  style of, 137, 140
coronations
  of Charles II, 144, 146
  Crown Jewels and, 7, 142–144,
    46–152
  of Elizabeth II, 2, 5, 7, 18–19,
    41, 22, 142–144,
    147–150, 152
  of George VI, 13, 147
coronavirus pandemic (2020),
    6, 11, 29, 117
Craig, Daniel, 182
Crawford, Marion, 35, 52,
    54–55, 172
Cromwell, Oliver, 146
Crown Jewels, 7, 142–144,
    146–152
Crown Ruby Necklace, 159
Cullinan Diamond, 144, 149, 151
Cullinan V Brooch, 164

D

D-Day commemorations, 11, 216,
    229, 233
Delhi Durbar Necklace, 156
Diamond Diadem, 142–143
Diamond Jubilee (2012), 29, 47,
    69, 112, 179, 197,
    14–215, 217, 228
Diana (princess)
  death of, 24, 29, 65
  family life of, 64
  jewelry worn by, 153, 158, 166
  legacy of, 85
  marriage of, 62, 67, 83, 203
Djokovic, Novak, 111

dogs, 170, 172–174, 177, 180,
    182, 184–185
Duke of Edinburgh's Award,
    33, 43

E

Edinburgh, Duke of, 32, 37.
    See also Philip (prince)
Edward (prince)
  birth of, 219
  childhood of, 42, 44–45, 59,
    61, 202
  family life of, 64, 223
  marriage of, 51, 66
Eisenhower, Dwight, 81
Elizabeth (princess). *See also
    Elizabeth II (queen)*
  animals and, 170, 172–173
  birth of, 12
  childhood of, 1, 5, 52–55, 194,
    206, 218
  christening of, 12
  courtship of, 32, 35–36
  death of father, 17, 40
  as equestrian, 172
  first public engagement of, 15
  first radio broadcasts by, 14–15
  jewelry worn by, 147, 153–154,
    162, 165
  in line of succession, 12–13
  marriage of, 37–40, 122, 154,
    57
  residence of, 40
  travels of, 16–17, 40, 75–76,
    78, 81, 98
  wedding of, 36–39, 122, 127,
    53–154, 157, 159,
    66–167
  World War II service of, 6, 8–9
Elizabeth (queen). *See also
    Queen Mother; York,
    Duchess of*
  balcony photo of, 218
  at coronations, 13, 147
  family life of, 53, 55, 78
  jewelry worn by, 159
  at King George VI's funeral, 18
  travels of, 21, 78, 81
Elizabeth II (queen)
  90th birthday celebration, 51,
    64, 135, 179, 230–231
  animals and, 168–171, 174–187
  Balmoral Castle and, 204

celebrities and, 94–117.
    *See also specific
    celebrities*
  charities of, 230–231
  commemorations and
    celebrations presided
    by, 29, 214–233. *See also
    specific commemorations
    and celebrations*
  coronation of, 2, 5, 7, 18–19,
    41, 122, 142–144,
    47–150, 152
  Crown Jewels and, 7, 142–144,
    146–152
  dancing and, 207
  death of father, 18
  on death of Princess Diana,
    24, 65
  as equestrian, 127, 133,
    168–171, 175, 177–178,
    181, 202. *See also
    specific equestrian
    events*
  family life of, 42, 44–45,
    48–51, 56–73, 177,
    188–189, 202. *See also
    specific family
    members*
  marriage of, 30–33, 41–47,
    223
  milestones of, 214–233
  music and, 206
  reign overview, 6–7
  royal duties of, 10–11, 19–29, 69
  royal residences of, 188–213.
    *See also specific
    residences*
  style of, 118–141. *See also
    fashion statements;
    personal jewelry
    collection*
  titles of, 98
  travels of, 74–93. *See also
    specific countries*
Epsom Derby, 164, 170–171,
    175, 181
Eugenie (princess), 97, 154–155,
    191

F

Fagan, Michael, 194
fashion statements. *See also
    Kelly, Angela; personal
    jewelry collection*
  about, 120–121
  coats, 115, 118–120, 129, 138
  coronation dress, 122, 142–143
  dresses, 128–131, 133–137
  fur, 129
  gloves, 120, 127
  hats, 115, 118–120, 124–125,
    127, 30–132, 134–135,
    138, 141
  headscarves, 123, 175, 179
  Launer handbags, 120, 126
  military dress uniform, 127
  repeat of outfits, 138
  shoes, 120, 132, 134
  tartan, 127
  trousers and jodhpurs, 133, 175
  umbrellas, 140
  wedding dress and jewelry,
    122, 127, 153
Federer, Roger, 111
Ferguson, Sarah, 83
Festival of Remembrance, 233
Fiji, 41
Fisher, Geoffrey, 37
Flanagan, Mark, 197
Flower Basket Brooch, 162–163
Ford, Gerald, 106
Francis (pope), 115

G

Garden of Remembrance, 91
George (prince), 51, 68, 70, 73,
    162–163
George III (king), 192
George IV (king), 152, 187,
    192, 199
George IV State Diadem,
    142–143
George V (king)
  balcony photos of, 1, 5, 194
  Crown Jewels and, 149
  death of, 12
  family life of, 52, 172
  hunting, 206
  jewelry gifted by, 167
  residences of, 208, 212
  surname of, 42
  travels of, 77

George VI (king)
  balcony photo of, 218
  coronation of, 13, 147
  death of, 17–18, 40, 200, 208
  family life of, 55, 78, 172
  jewelry gifted by, 160, 164, 167
  on Princess Elizabeth's
    marriage, 36–37
  residence of, 208
  travels of, 21, 78, 81

Germany, 92
Gibraltar, 87
Girls of Great Britain and
  Ireland Tiara, 157, 166
Golden Jubilee, 89, 224
Golden Jubilee Necklace, 156
Greville, Margaret, 154–155

H

Harry (prince)
  death of mother, 24, 65
  on Duchess of Cornwall, 67
  as equestrian, 171
  family life, 63, 66, 70
  on his grandparents, 42, 46,
    51, 67, 97
  style of, 140
  travels of, 85
  wedding of, 47, 71, 232

Hartnell, Norman, 121
Hawking, Stephen, 115
Hicks, Pamela, 173
Hillsborough Castle and
  Gardens, 191, 213
Hong Kong, 77, 86
Horse Guards Parade, 64,
  73, 232
horses, 168–172, 175, 177–178,
  181, 183–184, 186–187,
  202. *See also specific
  equestrian events*

I

Imperial State Crown, 2, 5, 7,
  144, 150–152
India, 82, 108–109, 147
investiture ceremonies,
  19, 60, 117
Ireland, 77, 91, 133, 191, 213
Irish Republican Army, 43
Israel, 91

J

Jamaica, 86
Japanese Pearl Choker, 166
Jardine Star Brooch, 164
Jewelled Sword of Offering, 148
jewelry. *See* Crown Jewels;
  personal jewelry
  collection
John, Elton, 112
John Paul II (pope), 98, 107, 128
Jolie, Angelina, 116
Jones, Tom, 112
Juan Carlos (king), 87

K

Keeling (Cocos) Islands, 79
Kelly, Angela, 121, 129, 131,
  133–134, 139, 141,
  145, 157
Kennedy, Jackie, 102
Kennedy, John, 102
Kenya, 17, 40, 85
Key, John, 185
Knatchbull, Nicholas, 43
Koh-i-Noor diamond, 147
Kokoshnik Tiara
  Greville Emerald, 154–155
  Queen Alexandra's, 157
Kuwait, 91
KwaZulu Dance Company, 105

L

la Grange, Zelda, 110
London Fashion Week (2018),
  119, 121, 139
Louis (prince), 68, 70
Lover's Knot Tiara, 158

M

Malawi, 85
Malta, 40, 77, 93
Mandela, Nelson, 87, 110
Maple Leaf Brooch, 145, 164
Margaret (princess)
  childhood of, 1, 5, 14, 32, 35,
    50, 53–54, 218
  death of, 200, 224
  at equestrian events, 61,
    123, 175
  family life of, 50, 56, 61
  jewelry worn by, 160
  marriage of, 61, 83

on the Queen's jewels, 145
  royal duties of, 56, 78, 102
  style of, 140
Markle, Meghan, 47, 70–71, 161,
  232. *See also* Sussex,
  Duchess of
Mary (princess), 173
Mary (queen)
  balcony photos of, 1, 5, 194
  family life of, 52, 55
  jewelry worn by, 156–158, 161,
    163–164
  at King George VI's funeral, 18

McAleese, Martin, 213
McAleese, Mary, 213
McCartney, Paul, 102
Middleton, Catherine "Kate," 68,
  85, 160, 227. *See also*
  Cambridge, Duchess of
Midgley, Claire, 196
Mirren, Helen (dame), 114
Monroe, Marilyn, 100–101
Moore, Ryan, 184
Moore, Tom, 117
Mother Teresa, 108–109
Mountbatten, David, 36
Mountbatten, Louis, 36, 43
Mountbatten, Pamela, 40
Mountbatten, Philip, 32, 34–37,
  39–40, 122, 153, 195.
  See also Philip (prince)
Mountbatten surname, 36, 42
Mountbatten-Windsor,
  Archie Harrison, 71
Mountbatten-Windsor,
  James, 66
Mountbatten-Windsor,
  Louise, 66
Mugford, Roger, 170, 174, 180

N

Nahum, Baron, 36
Neue Wache, 92
New Zealand, 21, 86, 122, 129,
  163, 165, 222
New Zealand rugby league
  team, 182
Nizam of Hyderabad Necklace,
  166
Nizam of Hyderabad Tiara, 159
Nott, David, 185

O

Obama, Barack, 25, 112, 123,
  182–183
Obama, Michelle, 112, 123
Oklahoma! (musical), 96
Olympic Games (1956), 123
Olympic Games (1976), 62, 180
Olympic Games (1992), 180
Olympic Games (2012), 182
Oman, 91
Order of the Garter, 21, 137
Oriental Circlet Tiara, 159

P

Pakistan, 82, 113, 147
Palace of Holyroodhouse, 191,
  195, 212
Palace of Westminster, 26
Parke, Mike, 39
Parker Bowles, Camilla, 67, 225.
  See also Cornwall,
  Duchess of
Parliament openings, 26, 122,
  141, 144, 151–152
Parvin, Stewart, 118–119, 121,
  34–135
pearl necklaces, 167
Pelly, Claude, 19
Pendry, Terry, 181
personal jewelry collection,
  152–167
  brooches, 145, 154, 162–164
  Greville Bequest, 154–155
  necklaces, 153–157, 159,
    165–167
  tiaras, 145, 152, 154–161,
    166–167
  wedding jewelry, 153–154

Philip (prince)
  animals and, 173, 184
  celebrity meetings, 102
  commemorations attended by,
    224, 230–231
  on death of King George VI,
    7, 40
  on death of Princess Diana,
    24, 65
  as equestrian, 42, 48–49,
    171, 178
  family life of, 42, 46–49, 55,
    61, 177, 202, 210–211
  gaffes of, 33, 89
  marriage of, 30–33,
    37–47, 223

residences of, 190, 204, 213
retirement of, 47
royal duties of, 32–33, 41, 46–47
state visits of, 16, 21, 79, 82–83, 89, 92–93, 98, 104, 106
style of, 137
titles of, 32, 37

Phillips, Mark, 83, 153
Phillips, Peter, 64–65, 129, 179
Phillips, Zara, 62, 64, 171, 179–180, 227
Pius XII (pope), 98
Prince Albert Brooch, 163
Proclamation of the Constitution Act, 46
Putin, Vladimir, 111

Q

Qatar, 91
Queen Elizabeth 2 (cruise liner), 20
Queen Elizabeth II Award for British Design, 121
Queen Mother. *See also* Elizabeth (queen); York, Duchess of
animals and, 177
birthday celebrations for, 64, 223
death of, 29, 61, 200, 224
at equestrian events, 61, 75, 181
family life of, 55, 61, 79
jewelry worn by, 18, 147, 154–155, 160, 163–164
residences of, 52, 204
style of, 140
Queen Mother's Crown, 147

R

Reagan, Nancy, 129, 178
Reagan, Ronald, 178
Remembrance Sunday, 219, 232
Republic of Ireland, 77, 91, 133, 191, 213
Rhodes, Margaret, 32
Rhys-Jones, Sophie, 66
Richard, Cliff, 112
Royal Albert Hall, 69, 233
Royal Ascot, 56, 131, 169–171, 173, 175, 177, 184, 186–187
Royal Lodge, 52, 55

Royal Variety Performance, 96, 102–103, 105
Royal Windsor Horse Show, 61, 123, 133, 164, 179
Royal Yacht Britannia, 76, 80, 83, 88
Ruby and Diamond Floral Bandeau Necklace, 154–155
Rush, Caroline, 119
Russia, 111, 156

S

Sandringham House and Estate, 50, 70, 129, 173, 184, 191, 206, 208–211
Sapphire Jubilee, 167
Saudi Arabia, 91
Science Museum (London), 27
Scroll Tiara (Cartier Halo Tiara), 160
September 11 terrorist attacks, 227
Silver Jubilee (1977), 21, 220–221
Simpson, Wallis, 13, 202
Sinatra, Frank, 102, 107
Sofia (queen), 87
Somerville, Philip, 124
South Africa, 78, 87, 165
South Africa Necklace, 165
South Yemen, 88
Sovereign's Orb, 148, 150
Sovereign's Ring, 147
Sovereign's Sceptre with Cross, 4–5, 149–150
Sovereign's Sceptre with Dove, 149
Spain, 87, 199
Spencer, Diana, 62. *See also* Diana (princess)
Starr, Ringo, 102
St. Edward's Crown, 144, 147, 149
St. George's Chapel, 21, 71, 200, 225
St. James's Palace, 17, 37, 115
Streisand, Barbra, 105
Succession to the Crown Act, 70
Sussex, Duchess of, 42, 71, 153, 202. *See also* Markle, Meghan
Sussex, Duke of, 41, 71, 202. *See also* Harry (prince)
Sydney Opera House, 84

T

Taj Mahal, 82
terrorist attack victims, 28, 227
Thaarup, Aage, 127
Thailand, 104
Tindall, Mike, 227
Topolski, Feliks, 36
Tower of London, 144, 146, 229
Townsend, Peter, 56
Treacy, Philip, 124
Trevor-Morgan, Rachel, 118–119, 121
Trooping the Colour, 40, 66, 73, 127, 135, 168–169, 171, 219, 226
Truman, Harry, 81
Trump, Donald, 159, 233
Trump, Melania, 233
Tutu, Desmond, 87
tweets, 27

U

United Arab Emirates (UAE), 84, 90–91
United States state visits, 25, 81, 9, 102, 106–107, 112, 123, 129, 132, 159, 178, 227, 233

V

Victoria (queen)
balcony appearance by, 194
Balmoral Castle and, 204
burial place, 202
Crown Jewels and, 147
Frogmore House and, 202
jewelry worn by, 156, 159, 163
music and, 206
reign of, 27, 216, 228
Victory in Europe Day, 218
Vladimir Tiara, 156

W

Warren, John, 183
Warwick, Dionne, 107
Wattle Brooch, 145
Weatherill, Bernard, 127
Wessex, Countess of, 66, 69, 120
Wessex, Earl of, 66. *See also* Edward (prince)
West Bank, 91

Westminster Abbey, 18, 37, 68, 122, 142–144, 223
Whitelaw, William, 194
William (prince)
death of mother, 24, 65
as equestrian, 171
family life of, 63–64, 66, 68–69, 73, 202
on his grandparents, 46, 51, 96, 177
proposal to Middleton, 85
residence of, 190
royal duties of, 91, 102
style of, 137, 140
wedding of, 68, 227
William IV (king), 147
Williams, Serena, 111
Windsor Castle. *See also* St. George's Chapel
about, 200–201
equestrian events and horse breeding at, 178–179, 181, 202
fire (1992), 6, 203
as the Queen's residence, 45, 91, 203, 208
riding at, 178
royal visits at, 112, 117, 123, 185, 203
wedding receptions at, 67, 232
during World War II, 14, 35, 53–54, 146
Windsor Great Park, 48–49, 63, 172, 200, 202
Windsor Guildhall, 67, 225
Windsor Home Park, 171
Windsor surname, 42
Wintour, Anna, 139
Women's Institute, 69
World Trade Center site, 227

Y

Y Bwthyn Bach, 52
York, Duchess of, 12, 194. *See also* Elizabeth (queen); Queen Mother
York, Duke of, 12, 194. *See also* George VI (king)
Yousafzai, Malala, 113

Z

Zayed bin Sultan Al Nahyan, 84

PHOTOGRAPHY CREDITS

AFP: 81 (bottom), 176

A. J. O'BRIEN: 35 (top)

ALASTAIR GRANT: 159 (right), 197

ANDREW MATTHEWS: 140 (Catherine white umbrella)

ANDREW MILLIGAN: 27 (bottom), 212 (bottom)

ANDREW MURRAY: 222

ANN RONAN: 172 (right)

ANTHONY DEVLIN: 116

ANTONY JONES: 181 (bottom)

ANWAR HUSSEIN: 61 (bottom), 63 (left), 66 (top), 66 (bottom), 89 (right), 107 (bottom), 112 (top), 123 (bottom left), 158 (top right), 213 (top), 223 (left), 224

APIC: 13

ARTHUR EDWARDS: 230

BENJAMIN WHEELER: 153 (bottom right)

BEN STANSALL: 184 (bottom)

BENTLEY ARCHIVE: 175 (bottom)

BERT HARDY: 122 (left)

BETTMANN ARCHIVE: 46 (top right), 74, 94, 104 (top), 160 (right), 166 (left), 174

BOB THOMAS: 178

BUCKINGHAM PALACE: 29 (bottom)

CENTRAL PRESS: 52 (left), 99, 122 (right), 127 (bottom)

CHRIS JACKSON: 27 (top), 69 (top), 70 (top), 72 (spread), 117, 118, 124 (2011 hat), 124 (2013 hat), 125 (2005 hat), 126 (2015 purse), 133 (left), 164 (bottom right), 184 (top), 201, 229 (bottom), 233 (top)

CHRIS WARE: 40 (right)

CORBIS HISTORICAL: 58

DAILY HERALD: 100 (spread)

DAILY MAIL/SHUTTERSTOCK: 86 (bottom)

DANNY LAWSON: 155 (bottom right), 212 (top), 232 (bottom)

DAVE CHAN: 24 (right)

DAVE THOMPSON: 112 (bottom)

DAVID CHESKIN: 180 (top right)

DAVID GODDARD: 209

DAVID LEVENSON: 179

DEAN MOUHTAROPOULOS: 67

DOMINIC LIPINSKI: 71, 136, 198 (top), 199

EDDIE MULHOLLAND: 124 (2011 feather hat)

EXPRESS: 36 (bottom)

FAIRFAX MEDIA: 84 (top)

FOX PHOTOS: 15 (top), 16, 19 (top), 34 (right), 39 (left), 41 (top), 41 (bottom), 44 (spread), 79 (top), 124 (1965 hat), 148 (top), 153 (left), 154 (left), 175 (top), 219 (top)

GETTY IMAGES: 56, 151 (top), 155 (top right), 225

HARRY TRUMP: 186 (spread)

HORST OSSINGER: 104 (bottom)

HUGH ROONEY: 213 (bottom)

HULTON ARCHIVE: 40 (left), 59 (bottom), 60, 82 (top), 86, 105 (top), 105 (bottom), 148 (bottom), 149 (top), 206 (top)

HULTON DEUTSCH: 150, 157 (left)

JAMES DEVANEY: 227 (right)

JANE BARLOW: 205

JASON BELL/CAMERA PRESS/REDUX: 163 (left)

JAYNE FINCHER: 64 (top)

JIM WATSON: 123 (top right)

JOE GIDDEN: 70 (bottom)

JOHN SHELLEY COLLECTION: 108 (spread)

JOHN STILLWELL: 24 (left), 29 (top), 90, 92, 140 (Queen pink umbrella), 140 (Queen yellow umbrella), 196

JONATHAN BRADY: 47 (bottom), 115 (bottom)

JULIAN FINNEY: 123 (bottom right)

KARWAI TANG: 161, 233 (bottom)

KEN GOFF: 221, 223 (right)

KEYSTONE: 17 (bottom), 20 (top), 37 (left), 38, 39 (right), 43 (top right), 48, 55 (bottom), 146, 195 (top), 218, 219 (bottom)

LEON NEAL: 210

LEWIS WHYLD: 25

LICHFIELD ARCHIVE: 46 (top left), 62 (bottom), 125 (1972 hat), 127 (top left), 207 (bottom)

THE LIFE PICTURE COLLECTION: 18 (bottom)

LISA SHERIDAN: 53, 54, 55 (top), 57, 59 (top), 172 (left), 188, 194 (right)

LUCAS JACKSON: 227 (left)

LYNN PELHAM: 82 (bottom)

MARK CUTHBERT: 125 (top 2015 hat), 133 (right), 134 (left), 135 (top), 138 (top left), 138 (top right), 138 (bottom left), 140 (Camilla umbrella), 159 (left), 183 (bottom)

DECEMBER 3, 2008

The Queen departs the Palace
of Westminster after delivering
her speech at the state opening
of Parliament. She is wearing the
Diamond Diadem, also known
as the George IV State Diadem.

HEARST
HOME

Copyright © 2021 by Hearst Magazine Media, Inc.

All rights reserved.

Cover and book design by William van Roden

Photo research and editing by Jennifer Newman,
Senior Visual Editor, *Town & Country*

Library of Congress Cataloging-in-Publication Data
available on request.

10 9 8 7 6 5 4 3 2 1

Published by Hearst Home, an imprint of
Hearst Books/Hearst Magazine Media, Inc.
300 West 57th Street
New York, NY 10019

Town & Country, Hearst Home, the Hearst Home logo,
and Hearst Books are registered trademarks of
Hearst Communications, Inc.

For information about custom editions, special sales,
and premium and corporate purchases, please go to
hearst.com/magazines/hearst-books.

Printed in China

ISBN 978-1-950785-09-4